The Vital Role of Visible Devotion

By

Darin Bowler

Printed in the U.S.A.

ISBN-10: 1484163400
ISBN-13: 978-1484163405

All Scripture quotations are taken from the King James Version of the Bible (unless otherwise noted).

All titles by Darin Bowler are available through major book retailers. Or call toll free 1-866-819-7667

A CreateSpace™ publication createspace.com/4252352

Edited by Kowana Luci

Cover design by Paul Povolni

To Cammie

(1969-2012)

Contents

.

Chapter One

Two Kingdoms; One Choice

Once upon a time there was a small group of travelers who were preparing to retire for the evening when suddenly they were surrounded by a dazzling light. They knew that they were in the presence of some sort of celestial being. And so with great anticipation, they awaited a heavenly message of great significance that they knew must be especially for them. Finally, the voice spoke, "Gather as many pebbles as you can. Put them into your saddle bags. Travel a day's journey and tomorrow night will find you glad *and* it will find you sad." After the light departed, they began to voice their shared disappointment and frustration. They had anticipated a grand revelation of a great universal truth that would perhaps enable them to create wealth, health and purpose for the world. But instead, they were given this menial and burdensome task that made no sense to them at all. However, the memory of the brilliance of their visitor gave basis for each one of them to pick up a small number of pebbles and drop them into their dusty saddle bags, (while *still* voicing their discontent). Finally they traveled a day's journey and that night, while making camp, they reached into their old, shabby saddle bags and discovered that every single pebble that they had gathered had become a brilliant, shining diamond! Now...they were *glad* that they had diamonds. But they were *sad* that they had not gathered more pebbles.[1]

Well, it is my hope (and confident expectation) that throughout the course of this book (journey) you *also* will stumble upon more than just a few pebbles, or "nuggets" of truth, that can one day make *you* very glad as well.

You see, the Word of God is filled with a variety of striking and vital truths which are commonly unnoticed and/or discarded by other people who simply aren't concerned about truth. But God has an infinite wealth of rewards in store for those who value a knowledge of His Word above all else. According to Jesus, only the wise man who "digs deep" will unearth that certain foundation that results in the saving of his house (see Luke 6:48). It is those rare and precious few who, like Job, esteem the words of God's mouth more than their necessary food who will be the ones that discover the deeper things of God (see Job 23:12).

You see, there are many people who are *familiar* with the Bible, and there are even some who have somewhat of a respect for it. But sadly, they too often opt to follow deceitful and false traditions instead of the clear commands of God. Time and again they habitually, repeatedly choose to believe and accept the mere words of men which have been vainly parroted and repeated for many years rather than the pure words of God Himself found in the Bible. But I am confident that the ideals and principles contained and presented in this book will soon turn out to be more than ordinary "pebbles" to seeking, humble and obedient hearts. I am confident that if you meekly continue through this entire discourse, you will discover a fine, fine quantity of spiritual and eternal "diamonds" of truth that you very likely have never beheld before. And the more of them that you keep and retain, the happier you will be at the end of *your* journey. So now, let the excursion begin…

In the Book of Exodus, we find perhaps one of the most well-known stories in the history of the

Bible: Israel's departure out of the nation of Egypt. For many, many years the nation of Israel had been in bondage and oppression as slaves in a foreign land. So God called and commissioned a man by the name of Moses to lead God's people *out* of the nation of Egypt.

Now, at first the king of Egypt resisted Moses and refused to let God's people go. So God began to send many awful plagues onto the land until the king finally conceded. And it was very shortly after their departure that they found themselves on the shores of the Red Sea with Egypt's military rapidly approaching from behind. You see, the king of Egypt had changed his mind about letting them go. And so, with nowhere to turn, God suddenly instructed Moses to extend his wooden rod over the sea. And the sea astoundingly divided right in front of them. And God's people walked safely through the parted waters. But when the Egyptian army pursued them, they were destroyed as the waters heavily cascaded down again (see Exodus 14).

So, here was the nation of Israel now safely rejoicing and celebrating on the other side of the Red Sea. It was no more slavery and no more Egypt! Now, it was at *this* point in time that God had a grand assignment set before Him. He was to now, by some means, transform this multitude of former slaves into a distinguished, holy, civilized nation. And so one of the first things He did was give them a law. This law (sometimes referred to as the Law of Moses or the Mosaic Law) consisted of over six hundred commandments that governed them in such meticulous matters as their diet, how to farm their land and how to dress, etc. The law also governed them in a variety of moral, civil, social and religious matters as well. And it was by their *obedience* to this exclusive set of commandments and ordinances that God would separate them unto Himself as a *very* unique people. Notice what God Himself said of this:

Ye have seen what I did unto the Egyptians, and how I bare you on eagles' wings, and brought you unto myself. Now therefore, if ye will obey my voice indeed, and keep my covenant, then ye shall be a peculiar treasure unto me above all people: for all the earth is mine: And ye shall be unto me a kingdom of priests, and an holy nation. These are the words which thou shalt speak unto the children of Israel (Exodus 19:4-6).

Now, naturally there would be some, throughout Israel's history, who would disregard or "make light" of God's laws. (There are *many* examples that we could consider.) However, at the same time, there were also *others* who would love, embrace and endeavor to follow God's laws *no matter what the rest of society did.* You see, in their minds God was their King. And His law(s) superseded any other thing in the entire world. Consider those three Hebrew children spoken of in the Book of Daniel chapter 3 for a moment. They were captive *foreigners* in a strange land. They were surrounded by a vastly different culture. They were amid several diverse customs, habits and traditions, etc. Now, they could have *very easily* just blended in and went with the crowd, right? But there was a deep-hearted conviction within them decreeing that God's kingdom superseded any other kingdom (or culture) in the entire world. And so they wouldn't bow before a false god, nor conform to the typical norms of another culture. Jerusalem was *still* their homeland and, in their minds, God was *still* their King.

What about Daniel? He was told, "In *this* kingdom we don't pray to *anyone* except the king!" But Daniel knew down deep in his heart that *this* was not *really* his kingdom. Yes, he was here in flesh and bodily presence, but his heart and his soul and his mind were still at home (in Jerusalem). God was *still* his King. And so he opened his window toward Jerusalem, knelt down on his knees and prayed three times a day like nothing ever happened. Why? It was because God's law and God's kingdom surpassed any other custom, habit, tradition, decree or culture on earth!

Now, here's a question: Shouldn't *we* be just as willing to embrace God's commands over worldly customs? Hebrews 11:3 tells us that God's *true* children confess (or acknowledge) that they are strangers and pilgrims on the earth. In other words they will understand that this natural world is not *really* their home. They will live, think and behave as foreigners (or strangers) on the earth. And whenever God's commands oppose the *world's* customs, God's Word will *always* come first. They were willing to abandon and relinquish their identity with *this* world in order to be identified with God in His world (kingdom). Again, shouldn't *we* be just as willing to forsake and disown the customs and fashions of *this* world, and embrace the truth of God's Word instead? And then, the Book of Hebrews goes on to tell us that *because* they were willing to set their affections on Him (God) and His Word above all else, "God was not ashamed to be called their God." You see, we (saved Christians) are *also* citizens of another kingdom. Our true homeland is a *heavenly* (or spiritual) Jerusalem:

But ye are come unto mount Sion, and unto the city of the living God, the heavenly Jerusalem, and to an innumerable company of angels (Hebrews 12:22).

In other words, we are *in* the world but not *of* the world. The Apostle Paul also tells us:

And be not conformed to this world: but be ye transformed by the renewing of your mind, that ye may prove what is that good, and acceptable, and perfect, will of God (Romans 12:2).

You see, we are not to blend in or "camouflage" with the society that we live in. The truth is that society actually needs to match up to God's ways. Not the church always trying to catch up to the world's ways. And according to Paul here, we need to show (this means to visibly reveal) what God's will is for people. We (true Christians) are to be role models or living examples of "subjects" in God's kingdom. That's called being holy. Being holy is still a valid New Testament command that is, sadly (and quickly), fading away. Paul also said this:

Beware lest any man spoil you through philosophy and vain deceit, after the tradition of

men, after the rudiments of the world, and not after Christ (Colossians 2:8).

We also need to take care that we don't carelessly misplace the spiritual "goods" that we now possess by foolishly endeavoring to pursue the vain, disobedient and empty customs and practices of the culture that we reside in. The Apostle Peter also declared:

But ye are a chosen generation, a royal priesthood, an holy nation, a peculiar people; that ye should shew forth the praises of him who hath called you out of darkness into his marvellous light: Which in time past were not a people, but are now the people of God: which had not obtained mercy, but now have obtained mercy Dearly beloved, I beseech you as strangers and pilgrims, abstain from fleshly lusts, which war against the soul (I Peter 2:9-11).

Notice that Peter here refers to *true* children of God as "strangers and pilgrims." This means that we are, in a sense, "outsiders" in the world. It may not always be pleasant but it is a spiritual reality and truth that we (true Christians) need to accept and appreciate. We truly are citizens and subjects of a *higher* kingdom than you will ever find anywhere on this planet. We have a *higher* calling than to be just like everyone else. We have our *own* king to please. We are trained in a *higher* curriculum than that of this common world. We are founded in a more pure philosophy than that of common humanity. This is a divine doctrine that we have received, live by and embrace. Ours is a noble cause. It is to be a people who are "zealous of good works." Notice what Paul said of the Lord, Jesus Christ:

Who gave himself for us, that he might redeem us from all iniquity, and purify unto himself a peculiar people, zealous of good works (Titus 2:14).

You see, we have a higher calling and a higher purpose than everyone else. It is to serve, worship and *obey* the one true God. He is our King. Heavenly Jerusalem is our true and *real* homeland. We are citizens of a higher kingdom! Now, again…do the commandments of our King take precedence over the customs of this culture? Are you primarily, first and foremost a North American occupant, or are you primarily, first and foremost a New Testament Apostolic?

Now, please don't get me wrong. We should love our country and thank God for it. We should pray for our president. We should vote, support our troops, defend our freedoms and die for them if we have to. But first and foremost we need to be one-God, Apostolic, children of God. But again, do the commands of God take precedence over the customs and trends of popular North American culture? Are you primarily, first and foremost a North American occupant, or are you primarily, first and foremost a New Testament Apostolic?

I can imagine some saying things like, "Oh, but you don't understand. I *love* Apostolic preaching as much as anyone...I *love* being in an anointed church service...I so thoroughly enjoy all of the beautiful music and singing...I believe Acts 2:38...I even believe in one God...In fact, I even believe in holiness...*within!*" Yes, it *is* much more effortless and less demanding to believe in holiness within. It's holiness *without* that we North Americans usually have a hard time accepting. But again, we have to ask ourselves: Do the trends of this culture supersede the commands of God? Allow me to imagine, again, some responding with something like, "Well yes...I *would* adhere to certain teachings of the apostles. I mean I *would*...it's just that, well, there's this one little problem...I would *really* stand out amidst my culture." Well it's true. Obedience to God's Word *will* diametrically oppose you to popular North American culture. But we need to choose which culture matters most to us.

In Matthew 24:12 Jesus said, speaking of the last days that, "…because iniquity shall abound, the love of many will wax cold." That word "iniquity" literally means "lawlessness." No restraints. No governing factors. No rules. It also alludes to individuals who believe that there should be no consequences for their foolish or immoral behaviors, etc. According to Jesus, in the last days, lawlessness and blatant disobedience will become very pervasive in society. I am seeing this attitude, or spirit, prevailing more and more in our culture. I am finding it more and more of a habit to double-check the intersection in front of me when my light turns green. It is really becoming *quite* common for a few "last second" stragglers to be rushing their way through the intersection after their light has already turned red. Look at how common it is becoming to see the latest riot or "protest" appearing in the news. They are occurring nearly daily all over the world. It's almost as if it's becoming a trend. Sometimes vandalism and *millions* of dollars of damage is the result and ghastly violence occurs over things as frivolous and trivial as perhaps a hockey game or a ball game. It was not like this only a few years ago. Lawlessness is growing more and more pervasive in our society. Rules are beginning to no longer matter to many people today. Also, any disciplinary measures or warnings or reprimands are now hysterically decried as "harassment." We are living in a world of lawless hearts. And…what's *in* the world can (and does) very easily creep into the church. I know it's not popular to hear these days, but obedience *still* matters. Jesus said:

If ye love me, keep my commandments (John 14:15).

The Apostle Paul added this profound statement:

If any man think himself to be a prophet, or spiritual, let him acknowledge that the things that I write unto you are the commandments of the Lord (I Corinthians 14:37).

Paul's writings are not man-made mandates or temporary traditions. They are commandments of the Lord. This changes things quite a bit, doesn't it? And the Apostle Peter said this:

Moreover I will endeavour that ye may be able after my decease to have these things always in remembrance (II Peter 1:15).

In other words, even after Peter's dead and gone and his bones are nothing more than dust in the ground, his writings (teachings) *still* apply. Statements such as these add much weight to the things that the apostles taught and wrote. Obedience to their teachings still matters today. Consider these enlightening statements as well:

But God be thanked, that ye were the servants of sin, but ye have obeyed from the heart that form of doctrine which was delivered you (Romans 6:17).

Paul was thankful that these Roman Christians *were* (past tense) the servants of sin. But they obeyed from their hearts the doctrine (teachings) that Paul delivered to them. This tells me that in order for us *also* to escape from becoming a servant of sin, then we too need to obey the doctrines that he delivered. The Book of Hebrews 5:9 tells us that God is the author of eternal salvation to all those that *obey* Him. This is not a promise granted to those individuals who foolishly choose to *dis*obey the Word of God. Again, obedience matters. Peter also said:

Ye have purified your souls in obeying the truth... (I Peter 1:22).

Do you want your soul purified? Obey the truth. The Apostle Paul also said these words:

And to you who are troubled rest with us, when the Lord Jesus shall be revealed from heaven with his mighty angels, In flaming fire taking vengeance on them that know not God, and that obey not the gospel of our Lord Jesus Christ (II Thessalonians 1:7-8).

These are some very serious warnings for us to not lightly esteem the things that we find written in the Word of God. Please do not allow the dangerous mindset of this present world that we dwell in to creep in and take over *your* mind. Love the Word of God. Love this Apostolic doctrine. Choose which culture (kingdom) matters most to you. Is it the kingdom of God, or the kingdom of this present world?

I want to share with you a brief quotation that so befittingly describes the imprudent thinking that is so pervasive in our culture today. It's a thought-provoking syndicated newspaper column written for the Chicago Sun-Times on June 8, 1979, by the late Mike Royko, (who reportedly, was not even a religious man). It went as follows:

"Year after year, a handful of suspicious-looking characters who call themselves "clothing designers" issue their commands: Wear your dress short and wear boots and look like a hooker. . . Now dress like a gypsy fortuneteller...Now look like a farm wife... Now wear spike heels...Now show your thighs. And every time the pimps of fashion give the word, all these "enlightened" female persons obediently trudge to the clothing store."[2]

What a perfect description of the impractical behavior of many people in our culture. I have to ask: Should we alter and revise the scriptural mandates of God in order to comply with the current opinions of our culture? Should we follow God's Word, only as far as the masses choose to follow them? Do we claim our current, modern society as our sole moral guide? Again, we need to choose which culture (kingdom) matters most to us. Is it the kingdom of God, or is it the kingdom of this present world?

You see, one major problem with the North American mindset is that it seems we always need to know *why* we should do something before we will do it. But the problem with that kind of thinking is that God's Word doesn't always tell us *why* we should do certain things, or why we should *not* do certain things. We need to just make an effort to have the attitude that says we are going to do what the Word of God says *regardless* of whether we always understand the reason behind every command or not.

I want to share with you a brief story that I shared in my earlier book *The Prudence Awakening.* It well illustrates an important point here:

There once was a king who was growing old and knew that it was coming time for him to choose his next successor. But instead of choosing one of his assistants or one of his own children, he decided to do something a little different. He called for all of the young people in the kingdom to come together at his palace one day. He said to them, "It has come time for me to step down and to choose the next emperor. And I have decided to choose one of you." The children were shocked! But the emperor continued. "I am going to give each one of you a seed today. Just one seed. It is a very special seed. I want you to go home, plant the seed, water it and come back here one year from today with what you have grown from this one seed. I will then judge the plants that you bring to me, and the one I choose will be the next emperor of the kingdom!"

There was one boy named Jonathan who was there that day and he, like all the others, received a seed. He went home and excitedly told his mother the whole story. She helped him get a pot and some planting soil, and he planted the seed and watered it carefully. Every day he would water it and watch to see if it had grown.

After about three weeks, some of the other children began to talk about their seeds and the plants that were beginning to grow. Jonathan kept going home and checking his seed, but nothing ever grew. Three weeks, four weeks, five weeks went by. Still nothing! By now others were talking about their plants but Jonathan didn't have a plant, and he felt like a failure. Six months went by, still nothing in his pot. He just *knew* he had killed his seed. Everyone else had trees and tall plants, but he had nothing. Jonathan didn't say anything to his friends, however. He just kept waiting for his seed to grow.

A year finally went by and all the youths of the kingdom came together again to present their plants to the emperor for inspection. Jonathan told his mother that he wasn't going to take an empty pot. But she encouraged him to go, and to take his pot, and to be honest about what happened. He felt sick to his stomach, but he knew his mother was right. He took his empty pot to the palace.

When Jonathan arrived, he was amazed at the variety of plants grown by all the other youths. They were beautiful, in all shapes and sizes. Jonathan put his empty pot on the floor and many of the other children began to laugh at him. A few felt sorry for him and just said, "Hey, nice try!"

When the king finally arrived, he carefully surveyed the room and kindly greeted the young people. Jonathan just tried to hide in the back. "My, what great plants, trees and flowers you have grown," said the emperor. "And just think, today one of you will be appointed the next emperor!"

All of a sudden, the emperor spotted Jonathan hiding at the back of the room with his empty pot. He ordered his guards to bring him to the front. Jonathan was terrified. "The emperor knows I'm a failure! Maybe he will have me killed!"

When Jonathan came to the front of the crowd, the Emperor asked his name. "My name is Jonathan," he quietly replied. All the children now were laughing and making fun of him. The emperor asked everyone to quiet down. He looked again at Jonathan, and then announced to the crowd, "Everyone, behold your new emperor! His name is…

Jonathan!" Jonathan couldn't believe it. He couldn't even grow his seed. How could *he* be the new emperor?

Then the emperor said, "One year ago today, I gave everyone here a seed. I told you to take the seed, plant it, water it, and bring it back to me today. But the truth is, I gave you all *boiled* seeds which would not grow. And every single one of you, except Jonathan, have brought me large trees and plants and beautiful flowers. When you found that your seeds would not grow, you substituted *other* seeds for the ones I gave you, didn't you? And Jonathan was the *only one* with the courage and honesty to bring me a pot with my seed in it. Therefore, he is the one who will be the new emperor!"[3]

As you may have guessed, I *really* like that story. You see, we need to have this same heart and attitude that Jonathan had. We need to do what's right and be obedient even when it doesn't make sense to our carnal, finite minds. I know that times come when some things may seem such a ridiculous waste of time and energy. There are times when we are doing what's right and we are doing what we are supposed to do but it all seems to no avail. It all seems for no real purpose or for no real reason. And perhaps we may even be mocked or criticized or ridiculed because of our submission to God and His Word. But please understand that God's Word is never given in vain. It exists for a reason. Remember these words in the Book of Isaiah:

For my thoughts are not your thoughts, neither are your ways my ways, saith the LORD. For as the heavens are higher than the earth, so are my ways higher than your ways, and my thoughts than your thoughts. For as the rain cometh down, and the snow from heaven, and returneth not thither, but watereth the earth, and maketh it bring forth and bud, that it may give seed to the sower, and bread to the eater: So shall my word be that goeth forth out of my mouth: it shall not return unto me void, but it shall accomplish that which I please, and it shall prosper in the thing whereto I sent it (Isaiah 55:8-11).

God's Word is never stated in vain. There is a purpose and a reason behind every word of God. And sooner or later we need to get to the point where we are going to obey our King no matter what the rest of society is doing. We are citizens of *another* kingdom. May God give us hearts that are set upon Him and *His* kingdom above any other.

Chapter Two

Beauties in the Eye of the Beholder

There once was a very wise man that was travelling in the mountains. One morning he found a most precious gem in the middle of a stream. A few days later he met another traveler, a poor woman, who was very hungry, so the wise man kindly opened his bag to share his food with her. When the hungry woman saw the precious stone inside of his bag she asked the man if he would give it to her. He did so without any hesitation. The woman then left, rejoicing in her good fortune. Now, she knew perfectly well that the stone was worth enough to give her security for an entire lifetime. But a few days later she began to feel very bad about her greed and selfishness so she came back to return the stone to the man. "I've been thinking," she said, "I know how valuable this stone is…but I want to give it back to you in the hopes that you can give me something even *more* precious." "And what is that?" said the man. "Give me whatever it is within you…that enabled you to give me the stone in the first place.[1]"

I really like that story. And I suppose that if there's anything to be gleaned from this little tale it would be an appreciation of how we *also* need to discern between what is true (spiritual) wealth and what is merely a superficial (external, temporary) wealth.

Remember, a healthy and blessed soul is *much* more valuable than *any* jewel in the entire world. And by the way, there *is* a "jewel" that is, in the sight of God, a great, great price. Do you want to know what it is? It's a person (or people) who fear, honor and revere Him. God actually refers to people of this sort as His "jewels." Notice what God Himself said:

Then they that feared the LORD spake often one to another: and the LORD hearkened, and heard it, and a book of remembrance was written before him for them that feared the LORD, and that thought upon his name. And they shall be

mine, saith the LORD of hosts, in that day when I make up my jewels; and I will spare them, as a man spareth his own son that serveth him (Malachi 3:16-17).

You see? A "jewel" (in God's eyes) is an obedient, humble, and God-fearing soul. And obedience to God's Word causes us to "shine." Notice:

Do all things without murmurings and disputings: That ye may be blameless and harmless, the sons of God, without rebuke, in the midst of a crooked and perverse nation, among whom ye shine as lights in the world (Philippians 2:14-15).

And so just as we need to be able to discern between true wealth and a superficial, temporary wealth, we *also* need to recognize and acknowledge the fact that there is such a thing as true (inner, spiritual) beauty, and there is also such a thing as an artificial (false, synthetic) kind of beauty. And who, really, is the final judge of true and false beauty? It is God of course. He is the Creator and Beholder of *all* things.

One thing that I often affirm is that what was normal for the Book of Acts should be the norm for Christianity today. The Book of Acts is our role model (blue print) for what the church should be today. The church of the first century was, in fact, a highly influential and very powerful movement. It was also characterized by many prevailing miracles and signs and wonders, etc. People were filled with the Holy Ghost by the hundreds. Souls were being baptized in Jesus' name, being converted to the Apostles' doctrine and were being saved on a day by day basis. The New Testament Church was a very widespread and recognized movement indeed.

But we need to be reminded of another fact as well. In spite of all of the power and growth, there was also much opposition, persecution and suffering. There was much sacrifice and even bloodshed. You see, truth will *always* have its fair share of enemies. And so a question arises then: What was it that kept the church so strong and thriving in the midst of such violent opposition? Well, it was a people who possessed an unrelenting, die-hard passion for **Truth.** They were *thoroughly* convinced that the doctrine of Jesus Christ and the apostles was rock-solid, unbending truth. And of course, this conviction of theirs *often* diametrically opposed them to their society. So, in reality, *we* really shouldn't be too awfully surprised, that even the Lord, Jesus Christ Himself experienced opposition as well. Notice these words of Jesus Himself:

But whereunto shall I liken this generation? It is like unto children sitting in the markets, and calling unto their fellows, And saying, We have piped unto you, and ye have not danced; we have mourned unto you, and ye have not lamented. For John came neither eating nor drinking, and they say, He hath a devil. The Son of man came eating and drinking, and they say, Behold a man gluttonous, and a winebibber, a friend of publicans and sinners. But wisdom is justified of her children (Matthew 11:16-19).

You see, Jesus knew what it was like to be called insulting and hurtful names. He also knew what it was like to have His teachings ignored and to be viciously ridiculed by *many* people. No matter what He said or did, He always had His share of critics. He couldn't make everyone happy, without offending some others at the same time. You see, not everyone respected or accepted Him. Notice also these words in the Book of John:

But though he had done so many miracles before them, yet they believed not on him (John 12:37).

In spite of the fact that He was literally Truth incarnate, and in spite of all of His miracles and His doctrine being so divine, He still knew what it was like to encounter and experience opposition and unbelief. And so because of this, we, the church of the 21st century, should not consider ourselves entirely exempt from comparable opposition and forces of unbelief either. Yes, there are literal "forces" (both natural and spiritual) which war and contend against truth. And so because of this, we need to be evermore diligent and passionately dedicated to the *original* doctrines of Jesus and the apostles like we never have been before. Notice a few passages of Scripture which address this:

Now the Spirit speaketh expressly, that in the latter times some shall depart from the faith, giving heed to seducing spirits, and doctrines of devils; Speaking lies in hypocrisy; having their conscience seared with a hot iron (I Timothy 4:1-2).

Preach the word; be instant in season, out of season; reprove, rebuke, exhort with all long suffering and doctrine. For the time will come when they will not endure sound doctrine; but after their own lusts shall they heap to themselves teachers, having itching ears; And they shall turn away their ears from the truth, and shall be turned unto fables (II Timothy 4:1-2).

But there were false prophets also among the people, even as there shall be false teachers among you, who privily shall bring in damnable heresies, even denying the Lord that bought them, and bring upon themselves swift destruction. And many shall follow their pernicious ways; by reason of whom the way of truth shall be evil spoken of II Peter 2:1-2).

Obviously, these men of God (the apostles) foresaw a day when truth would be commonly minimized, despised, abandoned and even outright *rejected* by many people who actually claimed to be "believers" in God. They (the apostles) also warned us that several false teachers would arise, and that many (not a few) would foolishly believe and follow them.

Now, the Book of Romans chapter 1:18 describes a *very* interesting type of people. It talks about a people who suppress (or hold) the truth in unrighteousness. There are people who know between right and wrong. They know to do right; way deep down, but they willingly suppress that knowledge of truth. They bridle it and keep it stifled so to speak. Notice also these words in the Book of II Corinthians:

But if our gospel be hid, it is hid to them that are lost: In whom the god of this world hath blinded the minds of them which believe not, lest the light of the glorious gospel of Christ, who is the image of God, should shine unto them (II Corinthians 4:3-4).

You see, there are people who *see* absolute truth with their *own* eyes. They see the same "black and white" commands that everyone else sees, yet, at the same time, nothing ever seems to connect in their minds. There's never a visible change or any type of conversion that seems to takes place. They have, according to the Word of God, what is called "blinded minds." The Apostle Peter *also* describes a similar type of people in II Peter 3:16. He describes individuals who "…wrest [twist] the scriptures to their own destruction" (see II Peter 3:16). In other words they twist, bend and contort the Scriptures to conveniently match and harmonize with their own personal preferences. After their own lusts (desires) they embrace teachers that say just *exactly* what they *want* to hear. It seems that their own self-will and personal desires matter more to them than the plain, obvious commands of the written Word of God. And that, my friend, is a dangerous ground to find oneself standing upon.

When I was a very young boy, of about 4 or 5 years old, something was wrong with me. I actually *liked* school! And I knew that school (kindergarten) started precisely at 12:00 noon. I was also fortunate enough to know precisely what 12:00 noon looked like on our clock. Both hands simply pointed straight up! How easy was that? So one day I came up with a brilliant idea! I decided to climb up high upon the chair that sat in front of the clock, and I simply, manually moved the hands to the 12:00 noon position. Ingenious! Then I quickly got down, and loudly yelled for my mom to tell her that we had better get to school right away. When she came into the living room she looked at the clock, and then looked at me rather oddly and asked me, "Did you move those hands on that clock?" I was dumfounded as to how she could ever know or even *suspect* such a thing!

You see, I blindly assumed that when *my* clock said 12:00, then it was undeniably 12:00! No questions asked! At this young age I had absolutely no concept whatsoever of the clock being synchronized with such "astronomical" dynamics as the rotation of the earth around the sun, etc. You see, just because *my* clock on *my* wall said that it was 12:00 did *not* mean that the sun and the earth suddenly aligned accordingly. No. Time and the universe remained stable and unchanged regardless of what *my* little clock on Parsons Ave. in Merced, California said.

Well, it's the same with the Word of God. We don't have the ability or the license to conveniently alter or edit it however we see fit. No. It is forever settled and established in heaven by God Himself.

For ever, O LORD, thy word is settled in heaven (Psalm 119:89).

You see, we can't "reach" the Word of God (so to speak). We can't reshape it, we can't manipulate it. It is unchangeable. Psalm 19:8 tells us that the commandment of the Lord is "pure." This means that it is not mixed or muddled or pliable. It is uncontaminated, it is right and it is true. Just as it is!

We, North American's are, in reality, a very fickle and self-willed type of people. It seems that the average North American has a *very* hard time fathoming a God who actually has expectations or demands. It is really, really hard for us to truly grasp the fact that God actually does have rules and commandments. The overwhelming majority of North Americans seem to believe that God only exists to comfort, pamper, and console humanity. We seem to only want a God who will fight our court battles. We only want a God that will solve all of our marriage and family problems. We want one that will fix all of our money problems. We only want to hear of the "blessings" that He has in store for us. We want to know of all of those wonderful promises that are rightfully *ours!* Give us a God that will keep us and our kids healthy and safe! Any God other than one who will do all of those things for us, well…He's just a theory in some peoples' minds. He's just some sort of a self-inspiring concept that some religious "fanatics" irrationally harbor deep within their psyches.

You see, many people cannot really grasp or accept a God who has rules and commands. In fact, it really doesn't even matter what the Bible says. If they don't want to do it, then, it's simply not going to happen. Now, don't get me wrong, many of them *do* in fact have a certain amount of confidence in the Bible. They will pray and go to church, etc. In fact, some of them even believe some pretty "heavy" and intense doctrines found within the Word of God. Why, they even believe in some of those more "eccentric" things that a lot of unbelievers in the world commonly scoff at.

For example: They believe in the creation. They have no problem at all accepting the fact that an invisible, almighty being (God) simply spoke, and matter (physical substances) instantly came into existence. They even believe the story of Moses and Israel miraculously crossing the Red Sea. They have no problem at all believing that God powerfully parted the sea right in front of them. They even believe in the virgin birth. They concede to and accept the fact that Mary miraculously became pregnant by the Spirit of God. In fact, some of them even believe in the rapture. Yeah! They really do believe that Jesus will one day appear in the sky and call all of His faithful servants up into the air to dwell forever in heaven with Him.

They have no problem believing these intensely weighty doctrines. You see, as long as it doesn't compel them to physically or personally make any visible, notable changes, they'll believe anything that the Bible teaches. They will emphatically declare this because it is, after all, in the *Bible!* They believe these things because they are *Christians!*

However, if the Bible ever compels them to make any personal (physical, visible) changes to our lifestyle, well...*those* Scriptures suddenly become inferior in significance and application. *Those* passages, all of a sudden, become topics of little importance and no real, concern. After all, God truly could not *possibly* be concerned about such trivial matters as our flesh or our attire. Come on now, get real! In fact, some of the more "serious" or shall we say "orthodox" ones will sternly endorse and sanction the magnitude of taking communion in the right spirit (attitude).

Let's briefly observe the Apostle Paul's dreadfully sobering instructions regarding one's attitude when taking communion. Notice these words in the Book of I Corinthians:

For as often as ye eat this bread, and drink this cup, ye do shew the Lord's death till he come. Wherefore whosoever shall eat this bread, and drink this cup of the Lord, unworthily, shall be guilty of the body and blood of the Lord. But let a man examine himself, and so let him eat of that bread, and drink of that cup. For he that eateth and drinketh unworthily, eateth and drinketh

damnation to himself, not discerning the Lord's body. For this cause many are weak and sickly among you, and many sleep (I Corinthians 11:26-30).

Apparently they really seem to have *no* problem at all believing that *physical* (natural) things can be divinely connected to *spiritual* things. Imagine that a scoffer approaches one of them and challenges them by saying something like, "Come on man, and relax. It's just bread. You don't have to be *so* serious and grave about all of this." They would soberly reply with something like, "Oh no. You don't understand! This bread signifies the body of Jesus Christ! It carries a heavy consequence with it if we don't properly revere or esteem it as the thing which it represents." They may get a response such as, "Oh come on, it's just a small shot of grape juice! Why all of the doom and gloom? Just gulp it down! Have seconds!" They would likely respond with some explanation of how it symbolizes the precious, soul-saving blood of Christ. They would explain how the *spiritual* significance of it makes it much *more* than just juice, and how it needs to be respected and treated as such. If not, well then…according to the Apostle Paul: "He that eateth and drinketh unworthily eateth and drinketh damnation to himself, not discerning the Lord's body. For this cause many are weak and sickly among you, and many sleep (die)."

So you see? They really seem to have *no* problem, apparently, believing that physical (natural) things *can,* in fact, be somehow divinely connected to spiritual things. And they seem to, with no trouble at all, accept the fact that there can even be some consequences if these physical (natural) things aren't properly esteemed or taken seriously.

However, if that physical (natural) thing happens to be their *bodies*…well…this changes things quite a bit! This now needs to be discarded and ignored before any hasty or irrational decisions are made. This becomes an issue of little concern and consideration.

You see, it's very interesting, however, that in the *very same chapter* that Paul talked about the significance of the bread and drink of communion, he *also* discussed the subject and significance of the length of a man and woman's hair. In fact, he hardly seems to have even rested his pen after teaching about it before he quickly moved on to the subject of communion.

Now…guess which one of these two subjects (communion or hair length) falls under heavy attack and much controversy when endorsed and encouraged to follow? Why, it is the one that dares to address our physical (personal) bodies, of course. Do you see what I mean then? How that as long as the Bible isn't compelling me to make any tangible, physical, notable changes to my daily living, then it's all right. As long as I'm not being instructed to make any personal alterations to my lifestyle, then His Word should be trusted and seriously heeded. But if He wants me to look different, or change my standard of living in some sort of visible fashion, then, well….that's just *your* interpretation. We don't need to take *that* part so seriously.

Before we go any further in discussing the subject of hair length in I Corinthians, first let's take a look at this short passage of Scripture in the Book of Ezekiel. This will help to serve as a basic foundation to our understanding of this topic. It is here (in the Book of Ezekiel) that we find a passage of Scripture where Satan is being reprimanded (rebuked) by the Lord Himself. Notice these words:

Thou art the anointed cherub that covereth; and I have set thee so: thou wast upon the holy mountain of God; thou hast walked up and down in the midst of the stones of fire. Thou wast perfect in thy ways from the day that thou wast created, till iniquity was found in thee. By the multitude of thy merchandise they have filled the

midst of thee with violence, and thou hast sinned: therefore I will cast thee as profane out of the mountain of God: and I will destroy thee, O covering cherub, from the midst of the stones of fire. Thine heart was lifted up because of thy beauty, thou hast corrupted thy wisdom by reason of thy brightness: I will cast thee to the ground, I will lay thee before kings, that they may behold thee (Ezekiel 28:14-17).

Notice here two things that Satan (Lucifer) lost many centuries ago:

1. A position of **covering** (as a hovering angel or "cherub" in God's holy presence).
2. His **glory** (his beauty, splendor, etc.).

Now notice *these* words in I Corinthians 11. Again, keep in mind that this is the *same* chapter (in the Bible) that discusses the solemn subject of communion.

Every man praying or prophesying, having his head covered, dishonoureth his head. But every woman that prayeth or prophesieth with her head uncovered dishonoureth her head: for that is even all one as if she were shaven. For if the

woman be not covered, let her also be shorn: but if it be a shame for a woman to be shorn or shaven, let her be covered (I Corinthians 11:4-6).

From this passage of Scripture we learn three things:

1. It is a shame for a man to prophesy or pray with his head covered.
2. It is a shame for a woman to prophesy or pray with her head *un*covered (a shame equal to cutting or shaving her head).
3. A woman should have a covering.

Paul said here that if a woman be *not* covered, let her also be shorn. In other words, if she has no head covering, it's just the same as having cut hair (being shorn). But if it's a shame for a woman to be shorn or shaven, then let her be covered.

Well, to find out for *certain* whether or not it truly *is* a shame for a woman to have cut hair, let us look to the Word of God. Is that not truly the best source for truth?

In the Word of God the cutting of a woman's hair, or to make her bald, symbolized shame, disgrace or a loss of glory. Notice these words in the Book of Isaiah:

Therefore the LORD will smite with a scab the crown of the head of the daughters of Zion, and the LORD will discover their secret parts (Isaiah 3:17).

To smite the head with a scab means to make bald with a disease. Notice this passage also:

And it shall come to pass, that instead of sweet smell there shall be stink; and instead of a girdle a rent; and instead of well set hair baldness; and instead of a stomacher a girding of sackcloth; and burning instead of beauty (Isaiah 3:24).

The Book of Jeremiah also sheds some light on this subject:

And I saw, when for all the causes whereby backsliding Israel committed adultery I had put her away, and given her a bill of divorce; yet her treacherous sister Judah feared not, but went and played the harlot also (Jeremiah 3:8).

In the above passage of Scripture, God's people (the nation of Israel) is depicted as an unfaithful wife. Now look at this passage just a few chapters later:

Cut off thine hair, O Jerusalem, and cast it away, and take up a lamentation on high places; for the LORD hath rejected and forsaken the generation of his wrath (Jeremiah 7:29).

The Lord symbolically commanded her to cut off her hair as a sign of her dishonor and shame.

Now, on the other hand, a woman's naturally grown hair is symbolic of the blessing of God. Notice these words in the Book of Ezekiel:

I have caused thee to multiply as the bud of the field, and thou hast increased and waxen great, and thou art come to excellent ornaments: thy breasts are fashioned, and thine hair is grown, whereas thou wast naked and bare (Ezekiel 16:7).

It is evident that there is indeed an element of shame associated with the removal (cutting) of a woman's hair.

Now back again to the Book of I Corinthians, let us look at the next few verses:

For a man indeed ought not to cover his head, forasmuch as he is the image and glory of God: but the woman is the glory of the man. For the man is not of the woman: but the woman of the

man. Neither was the man created for the woman; but the woman for the man. For this cause ought the woman to have power on her head because of the angels (I Corinthians 11:7-11).

From this passage we can *also* learn three things:

1. The woman is of (came from) the man.
2. The woman was created for the man.
3. Because of this, the woman ought to have "power" on her head (because of the angels).

Now, this teaching, or set of commands, (on the subject of hair length in I Corinthians) is beginning to hold a great deal more merit than a mere cultural tradition or a voluntary option. Apparently there is something *so* spiritually profound about a woman's hair that it actually bridges into the region of the supernatural (angelic) realm. Now notice the next few verses:

Nevertheless neither is the man without the woman, neither the woman without the man, in the Lord. For as the woman is of the man, even so is the man also by the woman; but all things of God.   Judge in yourselves: is it comely that a

woman pray unto God uncovered? Doth not even nature itself teach you, that, if a man have long hair, it is a shame unto him? But if a woman have long hair, it is a glory to her: for her hair is given her for a covering (I Corinthians 11:11-15).

The word *nature*, in the passage above, comes from the Greek word *phusin*. It literally means natural reason or following the instinct of nature or common sense.[2] In other words, natural, common sense (nature itself) teaches us that it is a shame for a man to have long hair. But at the same time it is a *glory* for a woman to have long hair. Again, this teaching is rooted in something much more weighty and significant than a mere, simple "cultural tradition."

So from *this* passage of Scripture we learn three things as well:

1. If a man has long hair it is a shame to him.
2. If a woman has long hair it is a **glory** to her.
3. Her hair is given to her for a **covering**.

It's very interesting to me how that those same two things that Satan lost (his **glory** and a role of **covering**) are now found spiritually represented in, of all things, a woman's long hair.[3]

The Apostle Paul drew from (utilized) three extremely unalterable factors as a foundational basis to support and endorse his teachings here on the hair length of men and women. They are:

1. The God-ordained order of creation (the roles of men and women)
2. The angelic realm
3. Nature itself

Remember also what Paul himself said of his writings. He said that his teachings are *not* mere opinions of meager man. They are in fact commandments of God:

If any man think himself to be a prophet, or spiritual, let him acknowledge that the things that I write unto you are the commandments of the Lord (I Corinthians 14:37).

In fact, Paul *also* stated at the very opening of this same epistle that his teachings (writings) here are intended *not* for the Christians in Corinth *only*. But his letter is, in fact, written to:

"...them that are sanctified in Christ Jesus, called to be saints, with all that in every place call

upon the name of Jesus Christ our Lord, both their's and our's" (I Corinthians 1:2).

Paul's teachings (writings) are to be seriously heeded by *every* Christian, in *every* nation, regardless of what time period they abide in. No one has the authority to say that these things don't matter. No one.

Now, as long as we're on the subject of examining how some "pick and choose" which Scriptures they will accept and which Scriptures they will not accept, let's go just a little bit further...but in a different direction now.

This next example, I believe, is going to be *very* enlightening to you (and perhaps even a bit amusing as well). You see, there are only *six* passages of Scripture, in the entire Bible, where you will find the words, **"Let it not be."** Only six. They are listed here, in order, as follows:

And God said unto Abraham, Let it not be grievous in thy sight because of the lad... (Genesis 21:12).

Now, I seriously doubt that there is any sincere Bible scholar or commentator in the entire world who would render the words of this verse, "Let it not be" to *really* mean, "Let it be." Do you? Of course not. Why that would completely reverse the original, intended meaning of the whole thought, right? Now notice the second one:

And he said, Let it not be known... (Ruth 3:14).

Now, again I seriously doubt that there is any sincere Bible scholar, or commentator, in the entire world who would actually render the words of this verse, "Let it not be known" to *really* mean, "Let it be known." I mean again, wouldn't that completely reverse the entire, original intent of the idea? Of course it would. Now look at the third one:

"...let it not be joined..." (Job 3:6).

No serious Christian would interpret these words, "Let it not be joined" to *really* mean, "Let it be joined." That would be ludicrous. Hold on, there's yet another one:

"...let it not be iniquity..." (Job 6:29).

Again, can you imagine a Bible scholar seriously trying to convince his students that the words, "Let it not be iniquity", here, should really be understood to mean, "Let it be iniquity."? Of course not. Again, it would reverse the meaning of the verse. Well, there's still another one. Are you ready?

"…let it not be once named among you…" (Ephesians 5:3).

No sincere believer would dare render these words, "Let it not be once named among you" to really mean, "Let it be named once among you…." This is speaking of fornication, etc.

Well, guess what? There's *one* more passage of Scripture left. And guess which verse (of these six) is *commonly,* without any compunction at all, totally reversed by your average North American "Christian?" You guessed it. It's the next one. It is a passage of Scripture where the Apostle Peter is instructing godly women on how to present themselves before others in the world. Notice:

Whose adorning let it not be that outward adorning of plaiting the hair, and of wearing of gold, or of putting on of apparel (I Peter 3:3).

All of a sudden, whenever the Word of God has the "audacity" to address such "flimsy" issues as our personal appearance or fashion choices, it "magically" seems to lose its divine inspiration! All of a sudden, when the Word of God says, "Let it not be," it *really* means…"Let it be!"

Yes, apparently, we've had it all wrong for these past twenty centuries. My friends, *today* this passage now *really* means, "Whose adorning *let it be* that outward adorning of plaiting the hair, and of wearing of gold…" Yes, go on ladies and gentlemen; just disregard these archaic, outdated ramblings of the Apostle Peter here. You see, he just didn't quite have an adequate and sufficient understanding of the grace of God like we contemporary "intellectuals" now have today.

Oh, and by the way, while you're at it, just go ahead and toss out the Apostle Paul's silly ramblings on this subject as well. You know the ones:

In like manner also, that women adorn themselves in modest apparel, with shamefacedness and sobriety; not with broided hair, or gold, or pearls, or costly array (I Timothy 2:9).

No, don't you worry about this today. You just keep on doing what *you* want to do. We're not supposed to be "legalists" you know. It's the 21st

century after all! [*I **really** hope my sarcasm is sensed here.*]

You would think that some people unabashedly suppose that two of the most prominent and key writers of the New Testament (the Apostle Paul and the Apostle Peter) must have somehow, perhaps slipped into some kind of momentary lapse of reason (or something of the likes) to dare address such "trifle" and "minor" issues as, of all things, our apparel and appearance. But remember, we have to keep in mind two *very* important passages of Scripture at this point. Keep in mind that Paul said:

If any man think himself to be a prophet, or spiritual, let him acknowledge that the things that I write unto you are the commandments of the Lord (I Corinthians 14:37).

Paul's writings are, in fact, commands of God. And also keep in mind what Peter said:

Moreover I will endeavour that ye may be able after my decease to have these things always in remembrance (II Peter 1:15).

Remember, even after Peter's dead and gone and his bones are nothing more than dust in the ground, his writings (teachings) *still* apply. Even in the 21st century.

Please understand and keep in mind that this is *not* some new, strange, outlandish, or bizarre doctrine being presented here. This was a commonly widespread, accepted and established teaching not only within Christianity for over 20 centuries, but it was also a common standard even within regular, secular North American culture as well. It was only within the past few decades or so has this doctrine begun to be questioned, disregarded and forsaken. This is a reputable, time-honored, godly and sound teaching being presented here. It's classic. It's orthodox. It's approved. It's Apostolic. And *that's* what separates us from everyone else in the world. It's our unbending, absolute insistence that this *is* the Word of God. And no one has the authority to dismiss it. Remember:

All scripture is given by inspiration of God, and is profitable for doctrine, for reproof, for correction, for instruction in righteousness (II Timothy 3:16).

Even if it diametrically opposes us to the common and carnal mindset of North American culture, we need to love and live by the Word of God.

Now…I know the common criticism that usually arises at about this point. It goes something like this: "Man…why do you *dwell* on all of this stuff?" Well…we don't *dwell* on it. It's just that we don't ignore it. However, when we do venture to address it, it is *then* that we are accused of "dwelling" on it. We just love the pure, original doctrine of the Lord Jesus Christ and His apostles because it's **RIGHT**. Our doctrine should *not* differ from that of the apostles.

You see, when you *really* do love truth, you love *all* truth. You love truth even when it opposes personal preferences and popular opinions. Let me graciously advise you to simply and sincerely pray for a deep-rooted and sincere love of truth…and just see where it leads you.

Chapter Three

*Body and Spirit
(Modest is Hottest)*

I would like to draw your attention to a very fascinating passage of Scripture. It is found in the Book of I Samuel:

For rebellion is as the sin of witchcraft, and stubbornness is as iniquity and idolatry. Because thou hast rejected the word of the LORD, he hath also rejected thee from being king (I Samuel 15:23).

It is quite astonishing to me that, according to the Word of God, rebellion is actually equivalent to (and one and the same) as witchcraft! This is *very* intriguing to me. Most of us would likely consider the practice of witchcraft to be one of the more severe or extreme expressions of defiance against God, right? Whereas rebellion, on the other hand, we may consider to be perhaps a much less serious offence. But I want us to see exactly how closely related these two sins actually are to each other, and in fact *why* they are essentially one and the same. For that, we must start at the beginning.

In Ezekiel 28 we catch a glimpse of the origin of Satan and his original splendid, glorious appearance. Notice these words:

Thou hast been in Eden the garden of God; every precious stone was thy covering, the sardius, topaz, and the diamond, the beryl, the onyx, and the jasper, the sapphire, the emerald, and the carbuncle, and gold: the workmanship of thy tabrets and of thy pipes was prepared in thee in the day that thou wast created. Thou art the anointed cherub that covereth; and I have set thee so: thou wast upon the holy mountain of God; thou hast walked up and down in the midst of the stones of fire. Thou wast perfect in thy ways from the day that thou wast created, till iniquity was found in thee. By the multitude of thy merchandise they have filled the midst of thee with violence,

and thou hast sinned: therefore I will cast thee as profane out of the mountain of God: and I will destroy thee, O covering cherub, from the midst of the stones of fire. Thine heart was lifted up because of thy beauty, thou hast corrupted thy wisdom by reason of thy brightness: I will cast thee to the ground, I will lay thee before kings, that they may behold thee (Ezekiel 28:13-17).

This passage of Scripture describes the beauty and splendor that Satan originally possessed until *iniquity* was found in him. This word *iniquity* literally means *lawlessness*. It means to have no rules or restraints. It means to be governed by self-will only. In a word: Rebellion. Notice also this passage of Scripture. Here we find the self-centered mind-set of Satan:

How art thou fallen from heaven, O Lucifer, son of the morning! how art thou cut down to the ground, which didst weaken the nations! For thou hast said in thine heart, I will ascend into heaven, I will exalt my throne above the stars of God: I will sit also upon the mount of the congregation, in the sides of the north: I will ascend above the heights of the clouds; I will be like the most High. Yet thou shalt be brought

down to hell, to the sides of the pit (Isaiah 14:12-15).

Notice the *self*-centered attitude of Satan:

- "**I will** ascend to heaven."
- "**I will** raise my throne above God."
- "**I will** sit enthroned on the mountain…"
- "**I will** ascend above the clouds…"
- "**I will** make myself like the most High."

Observe the exaltation of *self* above all else, "I will," "I will," "I will," "I will," "I will," No rules. No restraints. No governing factors. Just do what *you* want. In a word: Rebellion.

Now observe his tactic in the Garden of Eden. You might recall this familiar scene in the Book of Genesis:

Now the serpent was more subtil than any beast of the field which the LORD God had made. And he said unto the woman, Yea, hath God said, Ye shall not eat of every tree of the garden? And the woman said unto the serpent, We may eat of the fruit of the trees of the garden: But of the fruit

of the tree which is in the midst of the garden, God hath said, Ye shall not eat of it, neither shall ye touch it, lest ye die. And the serpent said unto the woman, Ye shall not surely die (Genesis 3:1-4).

Notice again: No rules. No restraints. No governing factors. Just do what *you* want to do. In a word: Rebellion. Also, get this: When Jesus abruptly called Peter "Satan" it was because Peter was manifesting this *same* type of attitude. Look at this little scenario:

From that time forth began Jesus to shew unto his disciples, how that he must go unto Jerusalem, and suffer many things of the elders and chief priests and scribes, and be killed, and be raised again the third day. Then Peter took him, and began to rebuke him, saying, Be it far from thee, Lord: this shall not be unto thee. But he turned, and said unto Peter, Get thee behind me, Satan: thou art an offence unto me: for thou savourest not the things that be of God, but those that be of men (Matthew 16:21-23).

You see, Peter here was manifesting that same attitude (spirit) that rises up in each of us at the very thought or mention of *suffering* or self-denial. And then it even states that Peter began to "rebuke" Jesus. Can you imagine that?! Picture in your mind the Apostle Peter actually pulling aside the Lord Jesus Christ and scolding Him. We can see now the degree of impudence that can arise within us when we are told to expect some unpleasant realities in life. "No way, Jesus, this just can't be. You're all wrong. Now let's just stop all this foolish talk of submission and suffering now... I'm a child of God after all!" And it was right in the midst of this self-serving, non-submitting outburst that Jesus abruptly looked at Peter and called him...Satan! Personally I believe that Jesus was, in actuality, rebuking Peter *and* the Devil at the same time here. But again, we can easily begin to see that fine, thin line that exists between rebellion and witchcraft. Notice also this passage of Scripture:

(For the weapons of our warfare are not carnal, but mighty through God to the pulling down of strong holds;) Casting down imaginations, and every high thing that exalteth itself against the knowledge of God, and bringing into captivity every thought to the obedience of Christ (II Corinthians 10:4-5).

You see, we are instructed here to oppose and to war against any spirit (attitude) that *exalts* itself against God. Notice this passage as well:

Wherein in time past ye walked according to the course of this world, according to the prince of the power of the air, the spirit that now worketh in the children of disobedience (Ephesians 2:2).

You see, Satan rules the unsaved world and his spirit is actively at work in people who disobey God.

Now I know that this next subject may be of a little unease for some, but please allow me to address it for a brief moment as it helps to lay a vital foundation for this topic at hand.

In 1966 a man by the name of Anton Lavey founded the Church of Satan. He also wrote a book entitled *The Satanic Bible*. He stated these following words: "Satanism is a blatantly selfish religion." Of the Church of Satan he wrote, "It is a temple of glorious indulgence." [1]

Well, after learning some of the things that I have learned, I must say that I certainly do agree whole-heartedly with that statement. You see, true Satanism, in its purest, "factual" form is indeed a "religion" that is *totally* centered and founded upon an existence of flesh-satisfying indulgence as a way of life. In fact, you may be quite surprised to know that many practicing "Satanists" don't even believe that Satan is a real or literal being at all. To them he is a figurative, fictional representative (a character) that symbolizes or represents self-indulgence. So, in its essential form, Satanism is a "religion" of doing whatever is pleasing and satisfying to *you* (with no regard for God or His Word). In a word: Rebellion.

Now get this, the official definition of the word *rebellion*, according to *Webster's New World Dictionary* is: "Defiance of any control."[2]

Wow, so now we can begin to see just exactly *why* rebellion and witchcraft, in the eyes of God, are so closely related to each other. In His eyes they are pretty much one and the same.

So you see, in reality, people really don't need to go through all of the hassle and ritual of donning black cloaks and hoods, etc. One really needn't go and purchase a new, bright and shining pentagram at their local "Devil Depot." You really don't even need to get initiated into your local witch coven...or really even practice witchcraft at all! All you really have to do is simply exalt *your* own will and *your* own interests above God's and...you're on Satan's side. Rebellion *is* as the sin of witchcraft.

Now, *true*, Apostolic Christianity, on the other hand, is quite contrary, and in direct opposition to this self-willed philosophy. Because at the very heart and core of *true* Christianity is an exaltation of *God* first, others second, and thirdly, a *denial* of self. Think not? Remember these words:

And one of the scribes came, and having heard them reasoning together, and perceiving that he had answered them well, asked him, Which is the first commandment of all? And Jesus answered him, The first of all the commandments is, Hear, O Israel; The Lord our God is one Lord: And thou shalt love the Lord thy God with all thy heart, and with all thy soul, and with all thy mind, and with all thy strength: this is the first commandment. And the second is like, namely this, Thou shalt love thy neighbour as thyself. There is none other commandment greater than these (Mark 12:28-31).

The two greatest commands are to first *hear* (understand) that God is one (and that He is to be loved with our whole heart, mind and soul). And the *second* greatest commandment is to love other people as we love ourselves. Wow, not too awful much is mentioned here about our own personal wills or our own personal preferences. Notice again this passage as well:

But he turned, and said unto Peter, Get thee behind me, Satan: thou art an offence unto me: for thou savourest not the things that be of God, but those that be of men. Then said Jesus unto his disciples, If any man will come after me, let him deny himself, and take up his cross, and follow me (Matthew 16:23-24).

You see, according to Jesus, if one wants to be a true and sincere follower of Him then one needs to follow after Him (follow His teachings and ways, etc.) and (here we go again), one must deny himself. Look at this passage as well:

I beseech you therefore, brethren, by the mercies of God, that ye present your bodies a living sacrifice, holy, acceptable unto God, which is your reasonable service. And be not conformed to this world: but be ye transformed by the renewing of your mind, that ye may prove what is that good, and acceptable, and perfect, will of God. For I say, through the grace given unto me, to every man that is among you, not to think of himself more highly than he ought to think; but to

think soberly, according as God hath dealt to every man the measure of faith (Romans 12:1-3).

You see, we are not to think too "highly" of ourselves. Instead, we are to have a new, transformed mind that is now preoccupied with, and centered upon fulfilling the good, perfect and acceptable will of God. Not the will of our own selves. Again, this is all quite contrary to the self-indulging philosophy of Satan, is it not? Notice what Paul says here:

Fulfil ye my joy, that ye be likeminded, having the same love, being of one accord, of one mind. Let nothing be done through strife or vainglory; but in lowliness of mind let each esteem other better than themselves (Philipians 2:2-3).

Children of God must endeavor to have humility (lowliness of mind). Not always proudly exalting and pleasing ourselves above and before everyone else. And we should also esteem each other as *better* than ourselves. Again, this is a self-sacrificing life-style that is expected of true children of God.

So, we can very easily begin to see then that the chief objection of the "Religion of Rebellion" (Satanism) is to satisfy, exalt and glorify *self*. While the chief objective of the "Religion of Christ" (Christianity) is to satisfy, exalt and glorify *God*.

Now, let's talk about this word *glorify* for a moment, shall we? What does it mean to glorify? To glorify means to exalt, to show honor to, or to pay tribute to.

Now, there are *two* main areas that we are supposed to glorify (show honor to) God. They are:

- In body
- In spirit

Look at what the Apostle Paul said of this in the Book of I Corinthians:

What? know ye not that your body is the temple of the Holy Ghost which is in you, which ye have of God, and ye are not your own? For ye are bought with a price: therefore glorify God in your body, and in your spirit, which are God's (I Corinthians 6:19-20).

According to the Apostle Paul here, we are to show honor to (glorify) God *both* internally *and* externally. We are to show honor to (glorify) God in both *body* and *spirit*. We are not to leave one out. One is not to be without the other. Paul also stated this:

Having therefore these promises, dearly beloved, let us cleanse ourselves from all filthiness of the flesh and spirit, perfecting holiness in the fear of God (II Corinthians 7:1).

Did you catch that? We are admonished once again that we need to utilize both our flesh (bodies) *and* our spirits in glorifying God. We are not to leave one out. Additionally, we are to perfect holiness, how? We are to perfect (endeavor to fine-tune) holiness in the *fear* of God. This means that we should make decisions pertaining to holiness based on, or considering the potential wrath of God, not carelessly taking our chances on the hopes that He won't care one way or the other. No, we must perfect holiness in the **FEAR** of God. Remember these words as well:

Wherefore, my beloved, as ye have always obeyed, not as in my presence only, but now much more in my absence, work out your own salvation with fear and trembling (Philippians 2:12).

Make decisions, pertaining to your relationship with God, from the perspective of *fearing* Him. Perhaps a major problem with many today is that they are making decisions in the *lack* of a fear of God.

So, according to these passages of Scripture, obviously God is, in fact, concerned about such "trifling" things as our physical bodies and our appearance. Remember also these words of Paul:

I beseech you therefore, brethren, by the mercies of God, that ye present your bodies a living sacrifice, holy, acceptable unto God, which is your reasonable service (Romans 12:1).

Now, the question arises: How (pray tell) do we glorify God in both body *and* spirit? Well, the absolute *best* way is by obeying the Scriptures that pertain to each. So why do we need to glorify God in body? Well, the human body is, in reality, quite sacred. It is entirely separate from all of creation. We (human beings) are made in the image of God. Now, being made in the image of God means *much* more than just sharing some sort of anatomical resemblance or similarity to God's appearance. No, it's much more than that. You see, we share a certain *dignity* with God that no other created thing does. In fact, there is even a certain spark of *divinity* within each and every one of us just because we are human. We are visible representatives of the one true God. Our bodies were specifically designed and created to house His Holy Spirit. We are designed to be the temples (sanctuaries) of God. As such, a certain responsibility befalls us to consult the Master of the house (temple) in how to properly display and present ourselves to the unregenerate world around us. Remember, in the kingdom of Satan, flesh is exalted *above* God. But in the Kingdom of heaven, flesh is submitted *to* God.

Now, in the Old Testament, God instructed Moses to build a tabernacle for which to house and "enclose" the Spirit of God. A flaming pillar of fire hovered above the tabernacle signifying the indwelling presence of the glory and Spirit of God. But in the New Testament, when believers were finally filled with the Holy Spirit, the Bible tells us that small flames of fire miraculously hovered above each of them as they were filled with the Spirit of God. This signified that Spirit-filled believers were now the new "temples" of God.

And when the day of Pentecost was fully come, they were all with one accord in one place. And suddenly there came a sound from heaven as of a rushing mighty wind, and it filled all the house where they were sitting. And there appeared unto them cloven tongues like as of fire, and it sat upon each of them. And they were all filled with the

Holy Ghost, and began to speak with other tongues, as the Spirit gave them utterance (Acts 2:1-4).

Now, way back in the Old Testament, when Moses was first instructed to build the tabernacle, God told him, "See that ye make all things according to the pattern that was shown to you on the mountain." (See Exodus 25:8-9 and Hebrews 8:5.)

In other words, God was telling Moses not to alter the tabernacle. Don't add to it. Don't re-design it. Don't modify it. Just make it how I say to make it. It is unlike any other structure or dwelling in the entire world. It houses my glory and my presence!

You see, it was the Spirit of God that was residing *within* the temple (tabernacle) that made it such an intensely grand edifice. It wasn't the mere structure itself.

Well, in the New Testament, God has also given *us* plain instructions on how to properly display and present His temple (us):

In like manner also, that women adorn themselves in modest apparel, with shamefacedness and sobriety; not with broided hair, or gold, or pearls, or costly array; But (which

becometh women professing godliness) with good works (I Timothy 2:9-10).

Now, let's briefly examine just a few words here to help us understand what Paul was actually saying in this passage of Scripture. The word *modest* means: appropriate, proper or decent. If there is such a thing as modest apparel then there *must* be such a thing as immodest apparel, right? We can't claim that immodest apparel doesn't exist. Decent apparel then would, of course, be clothing that does not overly expose the body or that doesn't sexually arouse, entice or tempt others around you.

Jesus claimed that it is wrong for a man to lust after a woman. I think then that He would be displeased with a woman choosing to noticeably wear attire that is designed specifically to intentionally attract the malicious sexual attention or interests of those around her. Now, the *world* may *love* it, and actually promote and encourage it quite a bit. But God, on the other hand, the King of *our* realm, instructs us to abstain from it.

Next are the words *shamefacedness* and *sobriety*. To have sobriety is to have temperance, moderation and a soberness of spirit and mind. It comes from the Greek word, (the language of which the New Testament was originally written) *sophrosune*.

To be shamefaced, which comes from the Greek word *aidos*, is to possess an entire demeanor that is void of flirtatious or seductive appearance and behavior. It is possessing and manifesting a bashful demeanor (manner) toward the opposite sex. It is being inclined to withdraw from undue male attention.[3]

Obviously then, wearing cosmetic paints or applying artificial colors to ones face is automatically, instantly *un*-shamefacedness. It is the exact *opposite* of possessing shamefacedness. It is in fact "proud-facedness."

Now, if you *really* stop and think about it, be honest, isn't it a tad abnormal to actually paint a living, breathing organism? Don't natural, living things already come fully loaded with their *own* natural glory and beauty? We don't paint trees or animals in order to enhance and improve their beauty, right?

Imagine an individual who decided to enter his yard (or home garden) into a local judging contest. And so he decided that, in order to ascertain that he secure the 1st prize, blue ribbon, he would, first of all, paint all of the huge rocks in his garden an assorted variety of blue, green and pink. And then he decided to coat those "drab" shades of grey and brown of the tree trunks with a bright, dazzling yellow!

Be honest, you know that this person would certainly lose the contest, right? The judges would be very disappointed with these crude attempts at enhancing nature. Why? It's because the *true* beauty of any living thing is...*the living thing itself!* We don't paint lilies or birds or chimpanzees or horses in order to make them *more* attractive. We don't paint polar bears or zebras in order to attempt to make them prettier. No, they are remarkably beautiful just as they are. They are naturally stunning precisely as God made them. We don't paint living organisms. The only things that need paint are dead (non-living), inanimate things; things like houses, cars and furniture, etc. But all *living* things come fully stocked, automatically loaded and overflowing with their *own* natural splendor and God-given loveliness.

And come on, be honest, it is *especially* strange (unnatural) if that painted living creature is, of all things, a human being! A person is the *only* life-form on earth that is made in the very image of God. If anything comes already fully stocked with an automatic, natural, built-in glory, it is certainly a human (woman).

The only splendor, or glory, that needs to emanate from women who "profess godliness", according to the Apostle Peter, is an **obedient**, humble, chaste, and holy behavior that "shines" forth as a by-product of the Holy Spirit of God dwelling within them:

While they behold your chaste conversation coupled with fear. Whose adorning let it not be that outward adorning of plaiting the hair, and of wearing of gold, or of putting on of apparel; But let it be the hidden man of the heart, in that which is not corruptible, even the ornament of a meek and quiet spirit, which is in the sight of God of great price. For after this manner in the old time the holy women also, who trusted in God, adorned themselves, being in subjection unto their own husbands (I Peter 3:2-5).

The word *conversation* in the passage above actually comes from the Greek word *anastrophe* and it literally means *behavior*.[4]

This is how, according to the Apostle Peter, the holy women of old (godly women in the Old Testament days) adorned themselves. And this is how Christian women *today* should *also* adorn themselves as well.

By the way, it *is* quite interesting that, when you observe a few passages of Scripture, it becomes quite apparent that God's people, in the Old Testament, as a general rule, commonly *did*, in fact abstain from wearing jewelry. Notice these passages from various translations of the Bible which point this out:

Therefore the sons of Israel putted away their adorning, from the hill of Horeb (onwards). (And so, the Israelites put away their adornment, from that day at Mount Sinai, and forevermore.) (Exodus 33:6) [The Wycliffe Bible].

And the Israelites left off all their ornaments, from Mount Horeb onward (Exodus 33:6) [The Amplified Bible].

So the sons of Israel stripped themselves of their ornaments, from Mount Horeb *onward* (Exodus 33:6) [The New American Standard Bible].

Therefore the people of Israel stripped themselves of their ornaments, from Mount Horeb onward (Exodus 33:6) [The New English standard Version].

So after that, they wore no jewelry (Exodus 33:6) [The Living Bible].

Again, according to the Word of God, the glory (appeal and beauty) that needs to exude from women who "profess godliness" (women who claim to be godly) is an **obedient**, humble, holy and chaste behavior (demeanor) that stems from the Holy Spirit of God dwelling within them. This is what is *true* beauty and of a "great price" in the sight of God. It is not synthetic, artificial facial colorings and adorning of oneself with gold, trinkets, pearls or costly array.

Remember, we must endeavor to glorify God both internally and externally (in body and spirit). Not internally *only*. If you are filled with the Holy Spirit of God, then you *are* a temple of God. And He is the one (not us) who decides and dictates the décor of His "house".

Chapter Four

The Doctrine of Separation

Occasionally, in the Word of God, you may have noticed that we (children of God) are sometimes likened to sheep. Now, sheep are really very vulnerable and defenseless creatures indeed, aren't they? Think about it. They can't run very fast. They're not very strong. They don't have sharp teeth or menacing claws. No, they really are rather helpless creatures. Also, sheep tend to wander and stray at times. And so without the watchful eye of a good and caring shepherd, they too easily and too often become prey to the predator. Remember this warning:

Be sober, be vigilant; because your adversary the devil, as a roaring lion, walketh about, seeking whom he may devour (I Peter 5:8).

If there's anything to glean from these words it's a disclosure of the fact that Satan literally roams this world seeking for those who have wandered dangerously far from the "path of righteousness" and who have ventured precariously into his hostile vicinity. These aren't *my* words, or the foolish ramblings of a frightened, unlearned or paranoid "legalist". Nope, these are the very words of the Apostle Peter himself. Be watchful; be alert because Satan is out to devour you.

Now, before we progress any further in this discourse, it would be very beneficial for us to reaffirm and acknowledge a very important, key and primary doctrine (teaching) found over and over again throughout the Word of God. And that is the reality that it is entirely normal and customary for *true* children of God to be found walking a different (spiritually safer) path than that of the rest of the world. It is known as the Doctrine of Separation.

First of all I want us to quickly observe just a few passages of Scripture to assist us in laying the foundation for this beautiful truth. Notice these words recorded in the Book of Mark:

And when he had called the people unto him with his disciples also, he said unto them, Whosoever will come after me, let him deny

himself, and take up his cross, and follow me. For whosoever will save his life shall lose it; but whosoever shall lose his life for my sake and the gospel's, the same shall save it. For what shall it profit a man, if he shall gain the whole world, and lose his own soul? Or what shall a man give in exchange for his soul? (Mark 8:34-37).

It is imperative that every person grasp and thoroughly understand that there is *nothing* more valuable than their own soul. According to the Lord Jesus Christ, just *one* human soul is worth more than the entire world. One lone, solitary human soul is worth more than all of the gold, all of the oil, all of the diamonds, and all of the real estate in the whole entire world.

Now, the reason *why* your soul is so important is because it's everlasting. It's undying. Our bodies will deteriorate and decay. But this consciousness, that we presently experience, will never end. It will go on forever in either heaven or hell. That's a terribly sobering thought, is it not? That is why your soul is so important.

Now, if our souls were only temporary and lasted only as long as our days here on earth, then they wouldn't hold quite the same value, would they? But the fact that they are eternal changes everything.

The fact that this present consciousness will never end changes the whole lot! There is nothing more priceless, in the entire world, than your own soul.

Now, the things we value, we protect, right? For example: We love and protect our children. Therefore, we buy them helmets to wear when they are out riding their bikes or skateboards. We want their pretty little heads to be padded and cushioned just as much as reasonably possible, right?

We tenderly strap our little infants and toddlers firmly and snugly into their car seats when we are going on trips in the car. We want them safe and secure in case we get into even a minor accident. Why? It's because we value them greatly.

What about our money? How many people do you know who keep their wallets and purses, all fully stocked with credit cards, cash and checkbooks, on their front porches at night? How many just casually toss them onto the front lawn when returning home from work at the end of the day? Not many, right? You see, the things that we value and cherish, we protect. So there is really nothing strange or "bizarre" at all about having self-imposed safeguards and barriers firmly established in order to protect us (or our possessions) from physical harm, loss or danger, right?

Well, just as we take precautionary steps in order to ensure our *physical* health and safety, we should be just as willing to take precautionary steps in order to help ensure our *spiritual* health and safety as well.

One of the main purposes, I believe, of the Word of God is to save our souls from harm or destruction (damnation). Look at what Solomon said:

My son, keep thy father's commandment, and forsake not the law of thy mother: Bind them continually upon thine heart, and tie them about thy neck. When thou goest, it shall lead thee; when thou sleepest, it shall keep thee; and when thou awakest, it shall talk with thee. For the commandment is a lamp; and the law is light; and reproofs of instruction are the way of life (Proverbs 6:20-23).

The Word of God is specifically designed and intended to save us from spiritual harm and peril. Possessing a close familiarity with, and intimate knowledge of the Word of God can grant you a little something that I like to call "Spiritual Safety."

You see, there are many people who are quite informed of and familiar with the Bible, but they just don't obey it. As stated earlier, they see the same plainly written commands that everyone else sees, but in spite of that, they seem to have voluntarily allowed their minds to be convinced that there is really an alternate meaning that just so happens to better accommodate their self-wills and personal inclinations. They have allowed the holy, written Word of God to become reduced to a status that is secondary to their own preferences. And again, that is a very dangerous state to find oneself in. Remember, Romans 1:18 talks about those who suppress the truth in unrighteousness:

For the wrath of God is revealed from heaven against all ungodliness and unrighteousness of men, who hold the truth in unrighteousness (Romans 1:18).

Sadly, there *really* are people who know; way deep down, that they should be doing things differently. Yet they suppress that knowledge, or ignore it, to the detriment of their own souls.

I think it's a good idea to honestly ask ourselves this question: "Am I, possibly, one of those people?" Please heed this bit of advice: When it comes to the written Word of God, do all that you can to ensure that you are walking in the correct way of the Lord Jesus Christ and His apostles. We shouldn't add to, or omit little words here and there that subtly reverse the original intent of God's Word, just to accommodate our personal wishes.

There exists a certain little tendency within the human race that is really quite common to all of us. And that tendency is that we too often put undue emphasis on *temporary* things while we practically ignore the most important *eternal* things. This is why an athlete who can run faster, hit harder or shoot a basketball better than most is paid multiple millions of dollars. Whereas a church that ministers and proclaims spiritual truths and enlightens people on how to be saved and properly live for God has to hold a "bake sale" in order to help cover expenses. Our priorities are literally upside down in our world. But we are instructed in the Word of God to think higher than and be wiser than the rest of general humanity. Notice these words written by the Apostle Paul:

While we look not at the things which are seen, but at   the things which are not seen: for the things which are seen are temporal; but the things which are not seen are eternal (II Corinthians 4:18).

There are two very important facts that we must always keep at the forefronts of our minds and be ever mindful of. They are:

1. We are eternal beings.
2. We have an eternal fate (heaven or hell).

Remember these sobering words of Jesus:

Enter ye in at the strait gate: for wide is the gate, and broad is the way, that leadeth to destruction, and many there be which go in thereat: Because strait is the gate, and narrow is the way, which leadeth unto life, and few there be that find it (Matthew 7:13-14).

Then said one unto him, Lord, are there few that be saved? And he said unto them, Strive to enter in at the strait gate: for many, I say unto you, will seek to enter in, and shall not be able (Luke 13:23-24).

Knowing these words above to be true, shouldn't we do all within our power to enter in at the narrow way and the straight gate? Jesus Himself said to *strive* to enter in. That means to actually make an effort or to fight (battle or attempt) to make it to heaven.

Take note: When it comes to the safety of our eternal souls, we had better not be found side-tracked or detoured seeing just how far we can wander from the path of righteousness that is so clearly drawn out before us by God's Word. According to the Lord, Jesus Christ Himself, we need to make conscious attempts and tangible efforts in keeping ourselves far from the destructive perils and sinful pulls of this natural life.

Now, before you accuse me of being an unlearned "legalist" who doesn't really understand the grace of God for suggesting such things, may I remind you also of what Solomon said of this? Notice these words:

A prudent man foreseeth the evil, and hideth himself: but the simple pass on, and are punished (Proverbs 22:3).

A prudent (wise, cautious) man sees the evil from afar off and he, what? He hides himself from it. He keeps a safe distance even from things which may merely have the *potential* for harm. But it's the simple (foolish, unwise) man who acts like there's no real cause to be concerned. He goes on as if there's no danger at all, and he is ultimately punished. We need to literally try to keep ourselves from spiritual harm. According to the Word of God we need to maintain a safe, straight lined course right through the center of the gates of heaven.

You see, your life is a gift from God. It's not a game. When it's over, it's really over. There is no "reset" button. And it is *here* and *now* that we decide the destiny of our souls. We must wisely utilize our time and energy to keep ourselves pure, right, holy and acceptable to God.

And so, it would actually be very wise to establish some good, strong barriers between us and the damnation of hell, so far and wide that we don't even come *close* to being lost. And this is known as the "Doctrine of Separation". The Doctrine of Separation is a valid, sound, biblical doctrine. No, it's not a popular doctrine, but it's sound and it's right!

Now let's just look and see what else the Lord Jesus Christ says about establishing some safe barriers in order to separate us from the dangers of hell:

And if thy right eye offend thee, pluck it out, and cast it from thee: for it is profitable for thee that one of thy members should perish, and not that thy whole body should be cast into

hell. And if thy right hand offend thee, cut it off, and cast it from thee: for it is profitable for thee that one of thy members should perish, and not that thy whole body should be cast into hell (Matthew 5:29-30).

My! It seems to me like Jesus was quite a holiness preacher, don't you think? Do you see what Jesus thinks of this doctrine of holiness and separation from the world? It seems to me that He's suggesting that we do whatever it takes to keep our souls safe from hell. It seems to me that He's suggesting here that we should let our flesh be inconvenienced a little if it keeps our souls safe and sound. Yes, Jesus was a holiness preacher. God endorses this doctrine of separation. He's all for spiritual health and safety. Apparently, we need to establish some barriers between us and hell so far and wide that we don't even come *close* to being lost. Notice what Paul said as well:

Wherefore come out from among them, and be ye separate, saith the Lord, and touch not the unclean thing; and I will receive you. And will be a Father unto you, and ye shall be my sons and daughters, saith the Lord Almighty. Having therefore these promises, dearly beloved, let us

cleanse ourselves from all filthiness of the flesh and spirit, perfecting holiness in the fear of God (II Corinthians 6:17-7:1).

Would you like to be received by God? Of course you would. Would you like to be a child (son or daughter) of God? Of course you would. Well, there's a stipulation that needs to be met before that can happen. According to the Apostle Paul here, we need to "come out from among them, and be separate."

You see, the world has a path that it walks, and the church has a path that it walks as well. The world and the church are on two separate paths, with two separate destinations. And we can't hook up with the world on one side, and God on the other, and still expect to arrive at the same destination. There has to be a separation between righteousness and unrighteousness; between holiness and unholiness. Hebrews 12:1 tells us:

Wherefore seeing we also are compassed about with so great a cloud of witnesses, let us lay aside every weight, and the sin which doth so easily beset us, and let us run with patience the race that is set before us (Hebrews 12:1).

Many times we are strongly tempted to conform to the world, and to be just *like* the world. Some people (and even some churches) believe that the more worldly they look (or act), the more influence they'll have on the world. But believe me, it doesn't work that way. A person who is *sincerely* hungry and who is genuinely interested and searching for truth is not attracted to or intrigued by worldly Christians. They are looking for something different than what they are immersed in day after day. They (serious seekers) expect to see a difference in the real thing. They need to see a difference in *you*. If they are sincerely hungry for truth they will actually be intrigued by your holy distinction. This is precisely why Paul said:

And be not conformed to this world: but be ye transformed by the renewing of your mind, that ye may prove what is that good, and acceptable, and perfect, will of God (Romans 12:2).

By *not* conforming to the world we are more able to prove (show, manifest) what God's *true* will is for people. You see, this idea of conformity *to* the world is a lie and a trick of the enemy to create a dead, powerless, non-influential church. When God calls us *out* of the world, He expects us to be different *from* the world. We must take precautionary, visible, tangible, noticeable steps and measures to help ensure the spiritual safety of our own souls. We need to love and appreciate this "Doctrine of Separation" and holiness.

Chapter Five

Why God Likes Many Skirts

There once was a young man who applied for a job as a telegraph operator. He answered an ad in the newspaper and went to the telegraph office to await an interview. Though he knew Morse code and was qualified in every other way, seven other applicants were also waiting in the large, noisy office.

He saw customers coming and going and heard a telegraph clacking away in the background. He also noticed a sign on the receptionist's counter instructing applicants to fill out a form and wait to be summoned to an inner office for an interview. He filled out the form and sat down to wait. After a few minutes, the young man suddenly stood up, crossed the room to the door of the inner office, and walked right in. Naturally the other applicants perked up, curiously watching and wondering why he had been so bold. They jokingly chatted among themselves and finally determined that, since nobody had been summoned to the interview yet, the man would likely be reprimanded for not following instructions and quite possibly be disqualified from the job.

Within a few minutes, however, the young man emerged from the inner office escorted by the interviewer, who announced to the other applicants, "Thank you all very much for coming, but the job has just been filled."

They were all confused and one man spoke up and said, "Wait a minute, I don't understand. We have been waiting longer than he and we never even got a chance to be interviewed." The employer responded, "All the time you've been sitting here, the telegraph has been ticking out the following message: 'If you understand this, then come right in. The job is yours.'"[1]

Obviously this young man knew something that the others simply did not know. He had paid very close attention to something that all of the others had missed.

In a similar parallel I have personally noticed and observed on different occasions, when modestly dressed and attired women of God are inquisitively observed in a somewhat questioning or curious manner as well. I've seen it happen numerous times. Perhaps they are in a group, strolling through a park, or a mall or they walk into a crowded restaurant. When unwary eyes suddenly meet them they are immediately scanned from head to toe. Sometimes it may prompt a small smile and precede a quick whispered comment to another nearby. Some may suppose that a godly, modestly dressed woman is perhaps a "novelty" of sorts. Perchance she is considered to be an unlearned or naïve lady who has adapted some strange belief system through ignorance or maybe through some kind of imposed or even a "self-binding" belief system. However, in reality, a Bible-believing, obedient and godly woman is just simply keenly aware of some very certain, precious and spiritual truths that others are simply *not* aware of. Like that young telegraph operator interviewee, she is simply more alert, tuned in, attentive and responsive to some *very* valuable (divine) instructions that *others* have blindly tuned out or ignored. Certain Bible verses that others perceive as unimportant, mindless, empty clatter (like the incessant tapping of a telegraph) a godly woman luminously observes, heeds and follows.

Now, I suppose that there are innumerable scores of people all across America who own Bibles. I presume that many people feel that it is a book that *at least* ought to be found lying somewhere around the house. There are also, of course, many Christians who own them as well. But I repeatedly wonder how seriously the Bible is actually considered and applied to many peoples' daily living. I am concerned that the Bible is *owned* by millions, but rarely is it seriously *heeded*.

By the scores, I can envision Bibles lying around in thousands of homes, on shelves or in cabinets, just setting there, stored with eternally infinite and invaluable, spiritual information and soul-saving instructions. Yet, they are casually cast aside and ignored, day after day after day.

Yet, at the same time, there are *others* who own Bibles too. But these others consider their Bibles to be *much* more than mere "conversation pieces" lying around the home. Oh yes. They actually read it now and then, and deeply desire to understand it and to live by it. And when they *do* actually read and observe the things written within, they then make serious attempts to apply those things to their day by day lives. And yes, of course, these rare few who do this are commonly criticized and ridiculed. And sometimes even by other so-called "believers," they are scorned and coldly dismissed as spiritually hopeless simpletons.

But truth be told, many times, obedient children of God are just simply more keenly aware of certain divine revelations that others have never even taken the time to consider or discover.

Now, as we venture through this chapter, I am confident that you will gain a fresh and even a new understanding and appreciation for some timeless directives that were once delivered by the Lord Himself.

One of the first and primary things that we need to realize, as children of God, is that we are called and commissioned to walk a different path than that of the rest of the world. We have already spent a considerable amount of time discussing that fact. But allow it to be assured and reaffirmed, once again, that separation from the world is indeed a sound, standard New Testament doctrine.

Now, this next subject matter that we are about to address in this chapter *technically* does not apply to or pertain to *all* women everywhere. This subject applies only to women who "profess godliness." It only applies to women who claim a devotion to God.

Now, allow me to briefly lay a very important foundation. As we know, God's people did not always live in perfect obedience to God. There were times when they existed in a rebellious or backslidden state. In Isaiah 28 we find such a period. God's people were steeped in much immorality and sin. In Isaiah 28:1-11 we find that the Lord is prophesying some rather severe judgments against His people. And the reason that God is pronouncing these judgments upon them is because of the detestable condition of sin that they had descended into. In verse 1 we find these words:

Woe to the crown of pride, to the drunkards of Ephraim, whose glorious beauty is a fading flower, which are on the head of the fat valleys of them that are overcome with wine (Isaiah 28:1).

In verse 2 it states that God's mighty hand will cast them down to the earth. In verse 7 it states:

But they also have erred through wine, and through strong drink are out of the way; the priest and the prophet have erred through strong drink, they are swallowed up of wine, they are out of the way through strong drink; they err in vision, they stumble in judgment (Isaiah 28:7).

This nation had descended so low into sinfulness, and had become so corrupt that even the priests and the prophets failed (were in error) in vision (receiving direction and messages from God) and they stumbled in judgment. These men who were supposed to be the leaders and the "role models," so to speak, had themselves become so drunk with wine that they failed to "tune in" to seek God and discern His mind and will on behalf of the people. Notice the gross and foul condition that they had descended to. Verse 8 tells us:

For all tables are full of vomit and filthiness, so that there is no place clean (Isaiah 28:8).

What a detestable condition that they had plummeted to. Now, I especially want you to notice a few words in verse 13. Notice:

But the word of the LORD was unto them precept upon precept, precept upon precept; line upon line, line upon line; here a little, and there a little; that they might go, and fall backward, and be broken, and snared, and taken (Isaiah 28:13).

This is *very* interesting. We must ask ourselves this question: How is it that God's Word, given to people "line upon line and precept upon precept, here a little and there a little," actually causes people to... *fall?* Well, God's Word is deliberately and intentionally interwoven throughout with very valuable nuggets of truth. Here a little and there a little. It is intentionally structured and arranged this way so that only sincerely interested (or curious) people will find and discover truth. The uninterested won't. Notice what Jesus Himself said of this in the Book of Luke. He said:

And why call ye me, Lord, Lord, and do not the things which I say? Whosoever cometh to me, and heareth my sayings, and doeth them, I will shew you to whom he is like: He is like a man which built an house, and digged deep, and laid the foundation on a rock: and when the flood arose, the stream beat vehemently upon that house, and could not shake it: for it was founded upon a rock. But he that heareth, and doeth not, is like a man that without a foundation built an house upon the earth; against which the stream did beat vehemently, and immediately it fell; and the ruin of that house was great (Luke 6:46-49).

Jesus said that a wise man will, what? He will "dig deep." A wise man will excavate. He will personally search and seek out and discover those precious precepts that are deeply embedded in the Word of God. Now notice what the Apostle Paul said along these lines:

Study to shew thyself approved unto God, a workman that needeth not to be ashamed, rightly dividing the word of truth (II Timothy 2:15).

The Apostle Paul gives a command here for people to *study* the Word of God. But what does the word *study* really mean? Well, it means to *look*, *read* and *learn* how to please God. We shouldn't just guess how to please Him. We shouldn't just go by our "feelings" when making decisions on how to please God. We shouldn't just take the advice of a "preacher" or blindly follow the crowd. No, we should *study* (look, read, and learn) how to exhibit and present ourselves as acceptable to God.

Now here is where it gets even *more* interesting. The noteworthy thing here is that this command to study God's Word (given above in II Timothy 2:15) is found in what is known as a "Pastoral Epistle." A Pastoral Epistle is simply a fancier way of describing a written letter (or message) in the New Testament that contains specific instructions especially for *pastors* on how to properly lead, shepherd and instruct God's flock (the church). There are actually three Pastoral Epistles in the Bible. They are: I and II Timothy and Titus.

Now, the Pastoral Epistles, of course, can be beneficially applied to *all* of us. There are some very vital and essential things contained within them that we all can gather. However, please keep in mind that they are *specifically* written for pastors. Pastors (or Bible teachers in general) *especially* need to take heed to this command to *study* God's Word.

You see, the ministry is actually given to us by God. God gave us (the church) pastors, teachers, evangelists, etc. in order to help perfect, or "fine tune" us in our relationship with God. If this doesn't quite set right with you, take it up with God, because it was His idea. Notice:

And he gave some, apostles; and some, prophets; and some, evangelists; and some, pastors and teachers; For the perfecting of the saints, for the work of the ministry, for the edifying of the body of Christ (Ephesians 4:11-12).

God gave these offices (positions) for the benefit and spiritual wellbeing of the church. We see here, in this passage of Scripture, that pastors (or Bible teachers) are instructed to present to you the pure, unadulterated, untainted Word of God. We are to give it to you *exactly* as it was first presented over 20 centuries ago. Nothing should have changed since. Notice what else Paul said of this as well:

And the things that thou hast heard of me among many witnesses, the same commit thou to faithful men, who shall be able to teach others also (II Timothy 2:2).

The same things that the Apostle Paul presented to Timothy, way back in the first century, are the *same* exact things that we (21st century Bible teachers) need to be presenting to people today. We are instructed to do all that we can to make sure that the same things that the apostles taught back then are the same things that *you* are taught today.

But wait, there's more! Notice also *these* words of the Apostle Paul:

Hold fast the form of sound words, which thou hast heard of me, in faith and love which is in Christ Jesus (II Timothy 1:13).

Wow! Did you get that? Paul just said here, in essence, "Every word that I teach, *keep* them as the pattern for sound teaching."

Do you want to teach sound doctrine? Then be a stickler for *every word* that the Apostle Paul himself utilized when he taught. Do you want to receive, learn and understand *sound* (correct and healthy) doctrine? Then be a stickler for *every word* that Paul utilized when *he* taught.

Paul again reaffirms that a *true* man of God needs to be always...

Holding fast the faithful word as he hath been taught, that he may be able by sound doctrine both to exhort and to convince the gainsayers (Titus 1:9).

Again, a true, (dependable and trustworthy) Bible teacher ought to hold fast (preserve, keep and retain) the original, faithful Word of God just *exactly* as it was first presented and taught by the Apostle Paul in the 1st century. Notice this passage as well:

Therefore we ought to give the more earnest heed to the things which we have heard, lest at any time we should let them slip (Hebrews 2:1).

Please understand, you are going to encounter and hear many voices and theories in your life as a child of God. You will be bombarded by a multitude of ideas and philosophies and opinions on the Word of God. But which ones should we *really* pay attention to and regard the most? Who should we ultimately heed above all of the others? Well, that was answered by the preceding verse. We ought to give the "more earnest" (serious, intense) heed to the things which we have heard from the apostles lest at any time we should let them slip.

So, if the Hebrew church, in the 1st century, was instructed to always pay *more* attention to the things that they heard directly from the apostles, above all others, then, common sense tells us that *we* should too, right? Notice this verse:

Look to yourselves, that we lose not those things which we have wrought, but that we receive a full reward (II John 1:8).

We are exhorted here to look to (examine) ourselves and make sure that we do not lose, or let slip those things that we have been taught or that we have received.

You see, generation after generation, century after century, the things that we teach today better match up word-for-word, verbatim with what the apostles taught. Our doctrine should *not* differ from that of the apostles! Keeping that in mind, let's recall Paul's commandment:

I will therefore that men pray every where, lifting up holy hands, without wrath and doubting. In like manner also, that women adorn themselves in modest apparel, with shamefacedness and sobriety; not with broided hair, or gold, or pearls, or costly array; But (which becometh women professing godliness) with good works (I Timothy 2:8-10)

Now, since we are commanded in the Word of God to study, examine, keep, preserve and retain every single, detailed and specific word that the apostles originally utilized in *their* teachings, in order for us to ascertain that *we* present and hold correct doctrine today, let's closely examine these two words: *modest* and *apparel*.

First we'll consider the word *modest*. It's actually quite interesting that the word *modest* appears only once in the entire King James Version of the Bible. Now, the Greek word, (the language of which the New Testament was originally written), that is translated *modest* in the King James Version of the Bible, is actually *kosmios*. It means orderly, well-arranged, decent, modest, a harmonious arrangement, or adornment.[2]

Modest apparel would then, of course, describe clothing that does not tightly surround or conform to the intimate, detailed shapes and curves of the body.

Jesus once said, "Whosoever looketh on a woman, to lust after her, hath committed adultery with her already in his heart." If it's possible to sin by merely looking at a woman, how careful a woman should be to not intentionally dress in clothing that does not immodestly or overly expose her body. This speaks of clothing that does not visually allure or arouse the interests or desires of a man that you're not married to. Immodest apparel often stimulates and sets in motion many lustful thoughts and imagery, etc. And, immodest clothing *also* displeases God. Therefore, women who "profess godliness" should, according to the Word of God, wear modest apparel.

But how can we *truly* decide and define what *modest* actually is? I'm sure if we were to ask people we would get all kinds of differing definitions, right? Well I've got good news for you. We don't have to guess. God has revealed in His word precisely what is modest and what is not modest. In the Book of Isaiah chapter 47 God is pronouncing judgments upon the nation of Babylon. At one point He is specifically reprimanding the *women* of Babylon. In doing this He tells them:

Take the millstones, and grind meal: uncover thy locks, make bare the leg, uncover the thigh, pass over the rivers. Thy nakedness shall be uncovered, yea, thy shame shall be seen: I will take vengeance, and I will not meet thee as a man (Isaiah 47:2-3).

Well, obviously according to God, whenever a woman bares her leg and allows her thighs to be uncovered it as at this point that her "shame" (immodesty) is being demonstrated or observed. This must be one of those passages of Scripture that the Apostle Paul was referring to when he stated that:

All scripture is given by inspiration of God, and is profitable for doctrine, for reproof, for correction, for instruction in righteousness: That the man of God may be perfect, thoroughly furnished unto all good works (II Timothy 3:16-17).

God gave us the Scriptures in order to help us more clearly and accurately define and explain what is right and correct. *All* Scripture is profitable for doctrine and for instructing us in righteousness. The Scriptures thoroughly furnish a true Bible teacher with the answers to many questions. We really don't have to guess *too* awfully much. But we *do* need to be informed of what the Word of God actually says now and then.

Well we've considered the word *modest*. Now let's look at this second word *apparel*. This word, translated *apparel*, comes from the Greek word (the language of which the New Testament was originally written) *katastole*. Now, this word *katastole* is very interesting too because it's the *only* time that *it* appears in the entire New Testament as well.

Now, the word *katastole* is what is known as a "compound word". It's actually a combination of two words combined together to form one word.

The Expanded Vine's Expository Dictionary of New Testament Words tells us that the first part of the word *kata* means *down*. This describes a specific garment flowing downward. And the second part of the word *stole* describes a long garment, covering or wrapping.[3]

So, when you put these two words together, *kata* and *stole*, forming the Greek word *katastole*, it specifically describes a very exact and particular *type* of clothing. It describes a downward hanging, loose garment (a modest skirt, or a dress, etc.). So, to put it all together, according to the Word of God, a godly woman's attire should be *kosmios katastole* or *modest apparel*. To put it in even plainer English: A modest, decent, downward, hanging, long (not short), appropriate dress or skirt.

You see, when God desired to describe how women who profess godliness (Christian women) should dress, He did not use generic, vague terminology. He described a very specific and precise type of apparel.

Now, isn't it a bit odd to you (or at least somewhat intriguing) that the Apostle Paul would specifically instruct Christian women to wear "downward, hanging, modest apparel", in the 1st century, when that's all that they ever wore anyway? Did it seem a bit funny or strange, perhaps, to his original readers in the 1st century, for him to specifically choose to use such a rare, yet very specific and rather "overly descriptive" word when describing what truly proper or modest attire is for women? Well, could it be that God foresaw a time, in the last days, when women would begin to forsake modest apparel? Could it be that God inspired the Apostle Paul to *specifically* use this very unique and uncommon word (katastole) for the sake of those rare few who would care to take the time and energy to

look, read and learn (study) I
think it's very likely.

Well, I suppose it \
complete to discuss this subject .
some elements of this next passage of ᴗ
well. Notice these words:

The woman shall not wear that which pertaineth unto a man, neither shall a man put on a woman's garment: for all that do so are abomination unto the LORD thy God (Deuteronomy 22:5).

From this passage of Scripture it is plain to see that God desires and demands a clear and visible distinction between men and women. This even includes the area of our attire and apparel.

Now, of course the New Testament plainly teaches that the Law of Moses (from which this passage above is derived) is now abolished. However, there is one element in this passage that still deserves our attention. It states that it is an "abomination" unto the Lord for a woman to wear that which pertains to a man. When an "abomination unto the Lord" is in view, there still remains a deeper underlying principle that needs to be considered. According to this verse, it is actually an "abomination unto the Lord" for a

113

to wear any thing that merely *pertains* (is
ed) to a man.

Now, of course one could easily shop around
for a more "modern" translation of the Bible which
would re-word this passage of Scripture above
(Deuteronomy 22:5) in a way that would lead a reader
to believe that actually all a woman should abstain
from is wearing a man's clothes. But the actual,
original words that God Himself specifically chose
are words that mean that women should abstain from
any thing that *pertains* to a man.

This is one reason why I *so* appreciate and
highly esteem the King James Version of the Bible.
The King James Version of the Bible is what is
known as a "formal equivalence" translation. This
means that it is a literal, word-for-word, verbatim
rendering of the *same* actual words that God Himself
used when conveying His words to the first, original
biblical writers. Many of these "modern" translations
of the Bible are what are known as a "dynamic
equivalence" translation. This means that the
translator is not so concerned about *every* literal word
of the original text, but is simply trying to convey
what *he* (the translator) personally *believes* that God
was *really* meaning (intending) to say. Thus, the mind
of the translator, then, becomes the final authority
instead of the Word of God itself. In actuality, when

one chooses to go by some of these "modern" translations, what they are actually doing is choosing to live by a mere *commentary* of the Word of God, and not the Word of God itself. [4]

Now, not many things are listed as "an abomination unto the Lord" in the Bible. The ones that are, are actually quite abhorrent sins. And honestly, it only takes a very basic and simple knowledge of the New Testament to quickly and easily reveal that those same things which were listed as abominations in the Old Testament, that are not specifically erased or removed in the New Testament (such as seen in Acts 10:15 and I Timothy 4:4), are still sins today.

By the way, as long as we're on the subject of abominations, I have often thought it somewhat interesting when I hear some who derisively claim that there is no New Testament command, given by Jesus Himself (or God), forbidding the sin of homosexuality. Well, in actuality, there really *is* a very plain New Testament warning given in the Book of Revelation. But you have to "do the math" to discover it. You see, in the Book of Revelation God Himself (or Jesus, the One upon the throne) states that the "abominable" (those who commit abominations) will not be saved. Notice this dreadful warning found in the Book of Revelation:

But the fearful, and unbelieving, and the abominable, and murderers, and whoremongers, and sorcerers, and idolaters, and all liars, shall have their part in the lake which burneth with fire and brimstone: which is the second death (Revelation 21:8).

Now, wouldn't it be quite cruel and heartless indeed for God to warn us that those who commit abominations will be lost, and then for Him to not tell us exactly what abominations are? Wouldn't it be kind of cruel to leave us to have to guess? But fortunately, we *are* informed, in His Word, what constitutes an abomination. And homosexuality is described as an abomination:

Thou shalt not lie with mankind, as with womankind: it is abomination (Leviticus 18:22).

So, when we "do the math," we see that there *is* in fact a New Testament warning given by God Himself.

Now, according to my knowledge, there is no culture or society, in recorded human history, where pants (trousers) were ever at one time considered to be the usual, accepted, normal attire for women.

Again, when it come: guesswork isn't a pru

But it really i, it? How that Deuterom wholly and perfectl teachings on "modes: Timothy? I Timothy uphold and sustain this

Now, let's take a quick look at this passage of Scripture in Deuteronomy again:

The woman shall not wear that which pertaineth unto a man, neither shall a man put on a woman's garment: for all that do so are abomination unto the LORD thy God (Deuteronomy 22:5).

I have heard it taught before that the word translated *man* above in this verse was actually erroneously mistranslated. It was claimed that the word *man* should *actually* have been translated as *soldier* or *warrior*. This teaching claims that God was simply forbidding women to wear the distinctively masculine armaments and articles of weaponry of a soldier. Well, I thought that was very interesting indeed. Until I found out that it was simply not true. You see, the Hebrew word (the language of which the

was originally written) that was
"man" is *geber*. The word *geber* is
man at least 48 times in the Old Testament.
once is it ever used to specifically describe a
der" or a "warrior". Whenever it is used, it is
only used to simply describe the generic reference to
a male person (a man) [5].

Let's just look at a few examples where this
occurs. Just mentally replace the word *man* in the
following verses with the words *solider* or *warrior* in
order to see how illogical this idea appears.

**And Job spake, and said, Let the day perish
wherein I was born, and the night in which it was
said, There is a man child conceived (Job 3:2-3).**

I don't know about you, but it seems a bit hard
for me to believe that Job was actually referring to
anyone proclaiming, "There is a *warrior* child
conceived tonight!" No, I think it was just a generic
reference to a male child in general. Notice this one
as well:

**There be three things which are too
wonderful for me, yea, four which I know not: The
way of an eagle in the air; the way of a serpent
upon a rock; the way of a ship in the midst of the**

sea; and the way of a man with a maid (Proverbs 30:19).

Yes, it is so wonderful and marvelous indeed to behold the way of a soldier (warrior) with a young woman! No, again this is obviously just a simple reference to a man in general.

With the merciful thou wilt shew thyself merciful; with an upright man thou wilt shew thyself upright (Psalm 18:25).

Ah yes, with an upright warrior (soldier) God will also show Himself to be upright. But you must be an upright soldier first! No, I think this is a broad-spectrum promise granted to all men whether they are in the military or not.

The steps of a good man are ordered by the LORD: and he delighteth in his way (Psalm 37:23).

Yes, the steps of a good warrior (soldier) are ordered by the Lord. But one must be a good warrior before the Lord will order your steps, you see. It's just too bad if a man's not a very good fighter. In that case, he's on his own. I suppose he *could* enroll into a local karate or kung-fu class in the hopes of attaining this wonderful promise from God. But there are no guarantees. No. Again, this seems to be a universal statement that applies to *all* God-fearing men in general. Not only to warriors.

Again, this has to be reiterated once more. This idea of women wearing distinctively feminine apparel (skirts or dresses) is *not* some new, strange, outlandish or "bizarre" principle that is being presented here. This was a commonly widespread, accepted, and established teaching not *only* within the religion of Christianity for over 20 centuries, but it was also a common standard even within the universal, regular (secular) North American culture as well. How did women dress only 50 years ago, or 60 years ago, or 70 years ago, etc.? Go on down the line as far as you wish to go. We know exactly how women dressed. All we have to do is look at history. They wore modest dresses and skirts.

And we have to honestly ask this question: *Why* did women dress the way that they did? It is precisely because of these passages of Scripture, in the King James Version of the Bible, that are being addressed in this discourse. That is why.

You see, for centuries the King James Version of the Bible had a profoundly positive influence upon *many* of the godly, moral qualities that once commonly prevailed in western civilization and North

America. And yes, it even influenced the modest attire of women in American culture. It was only within the past few decades or so has things began to change.

No, I am not presenting a strange, new or radical concept here by endorsing the distinctively feminine, modest, and godly attire of women. As a matter of fact, truth be told, it is actually a stranger and *newer* notion to attempt to eliminate it.

Again, if the Bible fails to serve as a sufficient source for authority on this subject, then just honestly observe our own American history. This is a reputable, time-honored, godly, and sound teaching that is being presented here.

In light of the abundance of information that has been presented in this chapter, it does become quite apparent that modest skirts and dresses are *still* the appropriate and modest attire that God desires on women who profess godliness. And again, when it comes to the state of our eternal souls, wishful presumption (guesswork) or taking our chances that these things *really* don't apply or matter today is not a wise or prudent option.

Now, I well know that there will be some who will claim that all of this "katastole" mumbo-jumbo is some sort of brainless expression of "overkill." I well know that there may be some who will claim that this much careful attention to detail is being *way* too "technical." Some may suppose that it dissects a little *too* deeply. However, this is precisely how God wants us to utilize His Word. It is a razor-sharp sword that slices very deeply into all of the microscopic details and affairs of the human life, psyche, and spirit.

For the word of God is quick, and powerful, and sharper than any twoedged sword, piercing even to the dividing asunder of soul and spirit, and of the joints and marrow, and is a discerner of the thoughts and intents of the heart (Hebrews 4:12).

We are to usefully and constructively apply the Word of God not *only* to external visibilities, but *also* all the way down to the littlest details and particulars of our innermost being.

And if (let me reiterate, *if*) you are of the opinion that all of this is too much attention to meaningless technicalities then here's what may be a major difference between me and you: I believe that *every word* of the Bible is inspired by God. You perhaps don't. And I also believe that *every word* of the Bible was accurately and successfully conveyed by God (to the apostles) intently for *our* admonition and instruction today. You may believe, on the other hand, that the Bible is merely the basic "gist" of what God was "trying" to say. But remember, even Jesus Himself said:

"...Man shall not live by bread alone, but by every word of God" (Luke 4:4).

Jesus claimed that we should live by *every* Word of God. Every word means every word. And Paul stated that:

All scripture is given by inspiration of God, and is profitable for doctrine, for reproof, for correction, for instruction in righteousness (II Timothy 3:16).

All Scripture (every part of Scripture) is given by *God*. It's not to be lightly esteemed or casually dismissed and discarded. Remember, Paul *also* said to:

Hold fast the form of sound words, which thou hast heard of me... (II Timothy 1:13).

He also exhorted:

And the things that thou hast heard of me among many witnesses, the same commit thou to faithful men, who shall be able to teach others also (II Timothy 2:2).

You see, we must faithfully endeavor to pass on and transfer the *same* words of the Apostle Paul that were written in the first century, to those who are hungrily seeking for truth today, in the twenty first century. And John benevolently instructed us:

Look to yourselves, that we lose not those things which we have wrought, but that we receive a full reward (II John 1:8).

You see, *every* word was personally "hand-picked," chosen and inspired by God Himself. And we (Bible teachers, Christians) are instructed to hold fast (keep and cling to) the very *same* words that Paul used back then as the pattern for sound teaching today. Yes, we are indeed called to walk a different path than that of the rest of the world. We live to please God and obey His Word regardless of what the rest of the world does.

Now, of course dressing modestly will not guarantee you a reservation in heaven. It will certainly not make you a "better" person than other people. But what it *will* do is display *obedience* to the Word of God. It will reflect a heart that is submitted to Him and a desire to dress "to the glory of God!" Remember these wise words of counsel given to us by the Apostle Paul:

Whether therefore ye eat, or drink, or whatsoever ye do, do all to the glory of God (1 Corinthians 10:31).

Chapter Six

His Workmanship

Before we journey further into this next topic we'll want to quickly observe a short yet very well-known and often quoted Bible verse. It is found in Ephesians 2.

For by grace are ye saved through faith; and that not of yourselves: it is the gift of God: Not of works, lest any man should boast. For we are his workmanship, created in Christ Jesus unto good works, which God hath before ordained that we should walk in them (Ephesians 2:8-10).

It's very interesting to me that in this passage of Scripture, Ephesians 2:10, we are called the workmanship of God. So, what exactly does it mean to be the "workmanship" of God? Well, the word workmanship means the by-product or the finished result of one's work or craft.

Imagine that you own a small bakery that specializes in wedding cakes. You would want to have the prettiest, best looking, best tasting and highest quality cakes in town, right? They're your workmanship! You would want to hire the best, most reliable and skilled bakers that you can possibly find, right? Why? It's because if all of the wedding cakes that your bakery makes are always slightly slanted and taste like celery, it makes you look bad, doesn't it? They're your workmanship! It's an embarrassment to you.

If you're a painter and all of your projects have thick, heavy runs of paint on them, it's a reflection of your skill as a painter. It's your workmanship! If a job or a product, that *you* produced, looks sloppy then *you* look sloppy. You appear slothful or incompetent in your skill (craft).

But on the other hand, if a job that you've performed looks first-rate, then you and your company look first-rate. It is *then* that you are respected and successful and in demand. Your workmanship is a by-product of your work.

Now, Ephesians 2:10 tells us that we are His (God's) workmanship, created to do good works. In other words, we are here to *obey* the Word of God and to *do* the will of God in order for us to *glorify* God. Notice what Paul said of this:

What? know ye not that your body is the temple of the Holy Ghost which is in you, which ye have of God, and ye are not your own? For ye are bought with a price: therefore glorify God in your body, and in your spirit, which are God's (I Corinthians 6:19-20).

Since we are no longer our own, but were purchased with a price (the precious blood of Jesus Christ) we now have a role to fulfill in glorifying God. We fulfill this role by submitting our bodies *and* our spirits to Him and His Word. And again, remember what Paul tells us in II Corinthians:

And that he died for all, that they which live should not henceforth live unto themselves, but unto him which died for them, and rose again (II Corinthians 5:15).

You see, we no longer live for ourselves but for Him (Jesus) who died for us. That's kind of a hard one for us to swallow, isn't it? We no longer live for ourselves, but for Jesus Christ. Notice these passages as well:

For it is God which worketh in you both to will and to do of his good pleasure. Do all things without murmurings and disputings: That ye may be blameless and harmless, the sons of God, without rebuke, in the midst of a crooked and perverse nation, among whom ye shine as lights in the world (Philippians 2:13-15).

God (through His Holy Spirit) is literally working within us, empowering us and assisting us in doing His good pleasure (His will). We should attempt to submit to Him and His Word without complaining and debating. When we live our lives in this manner we shine as light in the midst of a dark, cold world.

Let your light so shine before men, that they may see your good works, and glorify your Father which is in heaven (Matthew 5:16).

You see, according to God's Word, we are here to be visibly noticed and observed by the world. We are here to demonstrate what godliness is to a world that is *un*-godly. We are to exemplify holiness to a world that is *un*-holy. We are here to demonstrate and exemplify obedience to a world that is *dis*-obedient. We are here to shine as lights in a world that is dark.

So, how, exactly, do we do that? Well, we look at the Word of God, and make up our minds to do what it says. We listen to the man of God (the preacher) when he preaches and teaches the Word of God. And we make up our minds to do what the Bible says. We are not our *own* workmanship to do, look, and act however *we* want to. We are *His* workmanship.

In the Book of II Corinthians 5:20, the Apostle Paul tells us that we are "ambassadors" for Christ. An ambassador is a representative of the country (nation) that he (or she) comes from. An ambassador is supposed to dress the customs, speak the language, and be thoroughly knowledgeable of his homeland's standards, rules, and traditions, etc.

And so, in a similar (spiritual) parallel, we (children of God) are instructed to be living, visible representatives (or examples) of how *true* children of God should look and behave. A person who calls them self a Christian should be the *last* person on earth to be living in open, blatant, and defiant disobedience to the Word of God. Again, we are *His* workmanship.

I know that we are all made of mere flesh and blood. We all have certain weaknesses and faults. We are tempted, we make mistakes, we fall, and we battle. That's one thing. But it is something else entirely to voluntarily, purposely *choose* and to flat out *refuse* to do certain things that we *really* have the power to do. That's rebellion. And rebels are not on God's side. We are not our own workmanship. We are *His* workmanship, created to *do* good works.

Now, notice this very enlightening passage of Scripture in the Book of Mark:

And he began to teach them, that the Son of man must suffer many things, and be rejected of the elders, and of the chief priests, and scribes, and be killed, and after three days rise again. And he spake that saying openly. And Peter took him, and began to rebuke him. But when he had turned about and looked on his disciples, he rebuked Peter, saying, Get thee behind me, Satan: for thou savourest not the things that be of God, but the things that be of men. And when he had called the people unto him with his disciples also, he said unto them, Whosoever will come after me, let him deny himself, and take up his cross, and follow me. For whosoever will save his life shall lose it; but whosoever shall lose his life for my sake and

the gospel's, the same shall save it. For what shall it profit a man, if he shall gain the whole world, and lose his own soul? Or what shall a man give in exchange for his soul? Whosoever therefore shall be ashamed of me and of my words in this adulterous and sinful generation; of him also shall the Son of man be ashamed, when he cometh in the glory of his Father with the holy angels (Mark 8:31-38).

Now, I *especially* want you to notice these few words in verse 35 of the above text:

For whosoever will save his life shall lose it; but whosoever shall lose his life for my sake and the gospel's, the same shall save it (Mark 8:35).

Did you get that? Jesus just said here that whoever is willing to give up and forego certain little things in this life, for the sake of Jesus Christ and the gospel, will in reality be saving their own soul! Notice that He said, "For the sake of the gospel." We should be willing to make small sacrifices in this life, not only for the sake of God, but also for the sake of the gospel. Notice also this passage:

And when he was gone forth into the way, there came one running, and kneeled to him, and asked him, Good Master, what shall I do that I may inherit eternal life? And Jesus said unto him, Why callest thou me good? there is none good but one, that is, God. Thou knowest the commandments, Do not commit adultery, Do not kill, Do not steal, Do not bear false witness, Defraud not, Honour thy father and mother. And he answered and said unto him, Master, all these have I observed from my youth. Then Jesus beholding him loved him, and said unto him, One thing thou lackest: go thy way, sell whatsoever thou hast, and give to the poor, and thou shalt have treasure in heaven: and come, take up the cross, and follow me. And he was sad at that saying, and went away grieved: for he had great possessions. And Jesus looked round about, and saith unto his disciples, How hardly shall they that have riches enter into the kingdom of God! And the disciples were astonished at his words. But Jesus answereth again, and saith unto them, Children, how hard is it for them that trust in riches to enter into the kingdom of God! It is easier for a camel to go through the eye of a needle, than for a rich man to enter into the kingdom of God. And they were astonished out of measure,

saying among themselves, Who then can be saved? And Jesus looking upon them saith, With men it is impossible, but not with God: for with God all things are possible. Then Peter began to say unto him, Lo, we have left all, and have followed thee. And Jesus answered and said, Verily I say unto you, There is no man that hath left house, or brethren, or sisters, or father, or mother, or wife, or children, or lands, for my sake, and the gospel's, But he shall receive an hundredfold now in this time, houses, and brethren, and sisters, and mothers, and children, and lands, with persecutions; and in the world to come eternal life. But many that are first shall be last; and the last first (Mark 10:17-31).

Now, just like earlier, I want you to especially notice a few words in particular from the above text. Notice verses 29 and 30 from the above passage:

And Jesus answered and said, Verily I say unto you, There is no man that hath left house, or brethren, or sisters, or father, or mother, or wife, or children, or lands, for my sake, and the gospel's, But he shall receive an hundredfold now in this time, houses, and brethren, and sisters, and mothers, and children, and lands, with

persecutions; and in the world to come eternal life (Mark 10:29-30).

Now, in both of these passages of Scripture (Mark 8:31-38 and Mark 10:17-31) Jesus mentioned sacrificing, or going without certain things, for the sake of "the gospel." The "gospel" is the means whereby people (souls) are saved. The gospel is *very* important. It is the message of truth that explains to people how to be saved. It's the message of the plan of salvation. And Jesus is telling us here that we should be willing to suffer occasionally, or go without certain pleasures or personal preferences in order to promote and progress the gospel in our world. There is a beautiful and awesome example of this being demonstrated in action in the Book of Acts. Notice this little scenario:

And certain men which came down from Judaea taught the brethren, and said, Except ye be circumcised after the manner of Moses, ye cannot be saved. When therefore Paul and Barnabas had no small dissension and disputation with them, they determined that Paul and Barnabas, and certain other of them, should go up to Jerusalem unto the apostles and elders about this question (Acts 15:1-2).

Certain men crept into the church and began to teach that unless a man was circumcised, he could not be saved. When Paul and Barnabus caught wind of this doctrine they decided that they needed to meet with these men in order to settle this issue once and for all. Notice:

And when there had been much disputing, Peter rose up, and said unto them, Men and brethren, ye know how that a good while ago God made choice among us, that the Gentiles by my mouth should hear the word of the gospel, and believe. And God, which knoweth the hearts, bare them witness, giving them the Holy Ghost, even as he did unto us; And put no difference between us and them, purifying their hearts by faith. Now therefore why tempt ye God, to put a yoke upon the neck of the disciples, which neither our fathers nor we were able to bear? But we believe that through the grace of the LORD Jesus Christ we shall be saved, even as they...Wherefore my sentence is, that we trouble not them, which from among the Gentiles are turned to God: But that we write unto them, that they abstain from pollutions of idols, and from fornication, and from things strangled, and from blood (Acts 15:7-11; 19-20).

To make a long story short, it was finally decided and determined by the apostles and the Holy Ghost that a man doesn't need to be circumcised in order to be saved. Done deal. Settled. Case closed.

But notice something that happened just a little further down the road (in time that is):

Then came he to Derbe and Lystra: and, behold, a certain disciple was there, named Timotheus, the son of a certain woman, which was a Jewess, and believed; but his father was a Greek: Which was well reported of by the brethren that were at Lystra and Iconium. Him would Paul have to go forth with him; and took and circumcised him because of the Jews which were in those quarters: for they knew all that his father was a Greek (Acts 16:1-3).

The Apostle Paul, who had just battled certain Jews over this matter of circumcision being not necessary for salvation, now takes Timothy and…get this, he circumcises him! Now…what's up with that?! Now understand, Timothy did not subject himself to this ordeal in order to be saved. He knew Paul's teaching on this subject. So, why then would Timothy submit himself to such a painful (Jewish) ritual that no longer even held any spiritual significance? Well, he did it for the sake of the gospel!

You see, Paul and Timothy were trying to win and save Jews. Timothy's mother was Jewish but his father was Greek. And their (Paul and Timothy's) cause would be advanced and the Jews' reception to the gospel would be better enhanced if Timothy was circumcised. They were voluntarily choosing to do what would be best in order to reach souls for the kingdom of God. Now, all of this was done without even one single Scripture demanding it.[1] That's quite extraordinary.

Now, in light of this demonstration of intense, voluntary, non-required devotion to God, and the gospel, how guiltless do people stand before God when they *purposely* and *voluntarily* choose to ignore straightforward, simple and clear-cut commands of God that are revealed in His Word? How guiltless are people when they actually *see* and are made aware of plain commands of God, yet choose to ignore them?

Oh yes, we want our children to be saved. We want our relatives saved. We want to influence our world with godliness, morality and truth, etc. But how can *they* take the Word of God seriously if *we* don't take it seriously?

What doth it profit, my brethren, though a man say he hath faith, and have not works? can faith save him? If a brother or sister be naked, and destitute of daily food, And one of you say unto them, Depart in peace, be ye warmed and filled; notwithstanding ye give them not those things which are needful to the body; what doth it profit? Even so faith, if it hath not works, is dead, being alone. Yea, a man may say, Thou hast faith, and I have works: shew me thy faith without thy works, and I will shew thee my faith by my works. Thou believest that there is one God; thou doest well: the devils also believe, and tremble. But wilt thou know, O vain man, that faith without works is dead? Was not Abraham our father justified by works, when he had offered Isaac his son upon the altar? Seest thou how faith wrought with his works, and by works was faith made perfect? And the scripture was fulfilled which saith, Abraham believed God, and it was imputed unto him for righteousness: and he was called the Friend of God. Ye see then how that by works a man is justified, and not by faith only. Likewise also was not Rahab the harlot justified by works, when she had received the messengers, and had sent them out another way? For as the body

without the spirit is dead, so faith without works is dead also (James 2:14-26).

I believe that there are basically three ways to *truly* worship God. They are:

- In spirit
- In truth
- In the beauty of holiness

This is confirmed by the following verses:

But the hour cometh, and now is, when the true worshippers shall worship the Father in spirit and in truth: for the Father seeketh such to worship him (John 4:23).

Give unto the LORD the glory due unto his name; worship the LORD in the beauty of holiness (Psalm 29:2)

O worship the LORD in the beauty of holiness: fear before him, all the earth (Psalm 96:9).

These are the three areas of worship that we need to give our attention to in serving God: In spirit, in truth, and in the *beauty* of holiness.

Now, *beauty* is perceived and identified through the means of the eye, right? Therefore, the *beauty* of holiness must denote a physical and observable (visible) aspect of worship, right? Holiness is not limited *only* to our visible appearance but when familiarizing your self with the Word of God it becomes quite apparent that it *is* a vital part of it.

You know, honestly, I really don't think that Satan's top, urgent, and desperate priority is necessarily to blatantly shatter or totally annihilate every single fiber and minuscule (microscopic) aspect of our faith in God. No, in reality, all he *really* needs to do is just somehow influence us to be slightly off-balanced in our walk with God, (by omitting or neglecting *any one* of these three areas), and then we won't have a fully healthy and complete relationship with God. And you know...that's probably, to a certain extent, enough to satisfy Satan.

Remember, we are *God's* workmanship. We were created to glorify Him through good works; through our whole hearted devotion and obedience to His Word. We are not our own.

Chapter Seven

The Vital Role of Visible Devotion

I want to draw our attention to a certain prophecy that was uttered by the Lord, Jesus Christ:

And Jesus answered and said unto them, Take heed that no man deceive you. For many shall come in my name, saying, I am Christ; and shall deceive many. And ye shall hear of wars and rumours of wars: see that ye be not troubled: for all these things must come to pass, but the end is not yet. For nation shall rise against nation, and kingdom against kingdom: and there shall be famines, and pestilences, and earthquakes, in divers places. All these are the beginning of

sorrows. Then shall they deliver you up to be afflicted, and shall kill you: and ye shall be hated of all nations for my name's sake. And then shall many be offended, and shall betray one another, and shall hate one another. And many false prophets shall rise, and shall deceive many. And because iniquity shall abound, the love of many shall wax cold (Matthew 24:4-12).

I believe that we are living in days when iniquity is abounding and the love of many is waxing (growing, becoming) cold. Our world is increasingly becoming more and more violent and hateful.

At the same time, I also believe that it is becoming ever more difficult to simply keep God at the center of our lives. We are becoming ever more surrounded by "things" and activities and responsibilities and temptations to sin, that it actually requires an active discipline and a conscious effort to keep God at the very center of our lives.

Now, I want us to understand the fact that things we do in the natural realm can affect and have repercussions in the spiritual realm. Just consider all of the rebellion and immorality and sinfulness that is in the world because Adam and Eve took a bite of fruit. Physical actions can bring about spiritual consequences. Think not? Consider the eternal (spiritual) fate of those who simply receive a tiny, little thing known as the mark of the beast mentioned in the Book of Revelation:

The same shall drink of the wine of the wrath of God, which is poured out without mixture into the cup of his indignation; and he shall be tormented with fire and brimstone in the presence of the holy angels, and in the presence of the Lamb: And the smoke of their torment ascendeth up for ever and ever: and they have no rest day nor night, who worship the beast and his image, and whosoever receiveth the mark of his name (Revelation 14:10-11).

These are some pretty severe (spiritual) consequences being administered for merely receiving a small (physical) mark on the back of one's hand, are they not? After all, it's just a little mark, right?

Beginning at the Book of Genesis and all the way to the Book of Revelation we find example after example revealing the fact that physical actions can be connected and intertwined with spiritual actions.

Also throughout the Bible we find that obedience to the Word of God brings blessings and disobedience brings heartache and misery.

Now, sometimes obedience to the Word of God may seem like senseless rhetoric (in the natural realm of the flesh that is). But if it's done as an act of servanthood and genuine submission (worship) unto God, it can have profound, positive spiritual results. Knowing this to be true, it is so important that we take active, tangible, physical measures, and steps to ensure and ascertain that we are living in direct accordance to the Word of God. Remember, Jesus said that man doesn't live by bread alone, but by every Word of God.

We also observed how that Paul wanted every single word that he used to be permanently kept, preserved, remembered and carefully passed onto every believer, in every generation, on the face of the earth.

Hold fast the form of sound words, which thou hast heard of me... (II Timothy 1:13).

And the things that thou hast heard of me among many witnesses, the same commit thou to faithful men, who shall be able to teach others also (II Timothy 2:2).

Now let me forewarn you: When you endeavor to cling to every single Word of God, you are going to look different and act differently from everyone else in the world. This is because you truly believe that every word of this book that we call the Bible was inspired and given by God. Man didn't create it and man can't destroy it.

All scripture is given by inspiration of God, and is profitable for doctrine, for reproof, for correction, for instruction in righteousness (II Timothy 3:16).

Now, we, as human beings, with carnal (natural) minds have a difficult time remaining in a spiritual frame and state of mind 24 hours a day, 7 days a week. Let's be honest. There's times when we're neither in prayer nor even thinking any thing *about* prayer. There are times when we are not reading or meditating on the Word of God. There are times when we're not singing or praising God. There's times when all we're thinking about is where we can get some chocolate?! There are times when we're involved in a task at hand or at work. There's times when we are concentrating on an assignment at school. There's times when you are, perhaps, balancing your checkbook or driving (not at the same time, hopefully). There's times when we are shopping, or talking on the phone, etc. No, we do not live in a spiritual frame of mind every single waking moment of our lives.

But in spite of that fact, there are still some things that we can do in the natural (physical) realm that attest to the fact, 24 hours a day, that we are indeed worshippers of the one true God. There are certain choices that we can make and habits that we can acquire and lifestyles that we can adapt that *constantly* declare, 24 hours a day, to both God and man that we are children of God. They are visible, constant testimonies of our faith. Notice what Paul said:

Ye are our epistle written in our hearts, known and read of all men (II Corinthians 3:2).

An epistle is a written letter (or a message). So, according to this Passage, true children of God, who are endeavoring to live by the Word of God, are, in actuality, testifying or declaring, in a sense, how people ought to live. When we are living and manifesting a life of obedience to the Word of God we become tangible embodiments or living examples of how people truly *ought* to live. Remember what Jesus said:

Ye are the light of the world. A city that is set on an hill cannot be hid. Neither do men light a candle, and put it under a bushel, but on a candlestick; and it giveth light unto all that are in the house. Let your light so shine before men, that they may see your good works, and glorify your Father which is in haven (Matthew 5:14-16).

Our good works (obedience and conformity to God) need to be *seen*. They need to be literally witnessed and observed by the literal eyes of those around us. Yes, there are things that we can do in the natural realm *here*, that glorify God *there*, in heaven.

Now, at the time of this writing, our nation (The United States of America) is at war in Iraq. But we are *also* at war with each other. I believe that we, Americans are more divided right now than perhaps any other time in our entire history. But it's not a war of weapons; it is a war of ideals, morals, and principles.

You see, on one side we have what are called "conservatives." Conservatives believe that this country (America) was well-founded upon good principles and morals. Conservatives believe that this country is indeed the most blessed and powerful nation on earth. They believe that this is the case because of its past adherence to biblical (Christian) principles and standards.

On the other side you have what are generally called "liberals" or "secular progressives." They believe that America is a big problem in the world and is actually founded upon a flawed system of government. And they believe that it needs to be changed. Now, I very well know that I am using extremely broad definitions and explanations here. There may be some on one side who feel the same as others on the other side, on some issues, to some degrees here and there. I am simply presenting a very basic and easy-to-be-defined description.

Now, there are two very intense questions (issues) at the forefront of this present "war." They are:

- How should we handle terrorists?
- What role does God (or religion) play in this country?

Now, the traditional conservatives welcome public prayers and displays or mentions of God and religion, etc. However, the secular liberals, on the other hand, want little or no mentions of God and religion. And this battle seems to intensify and become more and more heated (and occasionally even hostile) through time.

Now, I have often stated that, what you see in the natural realm is often a direct reflection of what is happening in the spiritual realm.

When we saw Muslim terrorists fly planes into the Twin Towers, in New York City on September 11, 2001, we were also seeing, in the realm of the spirit, at the very core of it all, Satan attempting to obliterate Christianity. These men (terrorists) were merely natural, physical instruments, or tools utilized in an attempt to bring down, ultimately the church. On the surface it was Muslims trying to destroy America. But underneath it all, at the heart and core of it all, was Satan trying to crush Christianity.

You see, there is a *very* close connection between American patriotism and Christianity. This is so because this nation was rooted and established on the truths and principles of the Word of God, the Bible. This is *clearly* discerned and overwhelmingly confirmed, over and over, when you become familiar with *many* of the founding documents and charters, etc. that started this country. It really is an embarrassing revelation and exposure to one's ignorance when this idea is challenged or denied.

But you see, there is a spirit (or a force) that is at work in this nation (and the world) that is trying to create a society that is completely void of the biblical and traditional definitions of what is right and moral or "Christian." And this spirit is known, not surprisingly, as "the spirit of *Anti*-Christ." Notice what the Apostle John said of this:

"...And this is that spirit of antichrist, whereof ye have heard that it should come; and even now already is it in the world" (I John 4:3).

This "spirit" endeavors to glorify and exalt things that are foul, immoral, base and wrong. And, at the same time, it attempts to degrade and vilify things that are holy, clean, pure and right. This "spirit" (the spirit of Anti-Christ) is trying to re-align and reverse our society's thinking.

This "spirit" doesn't like definitions of what is normal and what is *not* normal. It doesn't like definitions of what is right and what is *not* right. It doesn't like definitions of what is good and what is bad. It seeks to create a culture that normalizes and accepts strange and abnormal behaviors and practices. And this "spirit," even though it is invisible, manifests itself in several, physical and visible ways. It cultivates and influences certain "trends" and

152

behaviors *specifically* for the purpose of trying to make the point that there is no authority, and that God is irrelevant.

This "spirit" expresses itself in the form of many different, nonstandard behaviors. It is expressed in the differing sexual deviancies that are becoming pervasive more and more today. God stands against the sin of homosexuality; therefore homosexuality is proudly flaunted and encouraged passionately.

It is seen in these wild, bizarre tattoos that cover the entire portions of people's bodies. It is seen in body piercings of all sorts. God spoke against such markings in the Old Testament. Maybe I'm a dupe, but I would think if He didn't like it then, then He doesn't like it now. Maybe I'm "dim," but I don't play Russian roulette either. And I *sure* wouldn't want to play it with my soul.

You see, God-given common sense and even nature itself tells us that it's *not* "normal" to stick metal through our tongues, our faces, eyebrows, noses, or our bodies. It's absurd to even *try* to support and defend it as "normal." It's *not* normal...and that, my friends, is *precisely* why it's done. It is done to visibly, physically make the point that there is no "right" and there is no "wrong." I wonder how many poor souls submit themselves to clownish, absurd and even physically painful ordeals just so they can feel identified or linked with others in society.

Imagine this scenario: "Hey look Alice, I got a chrome plated, metal peg going right through the center of my tongue!"

Alice replies, "Ewww…oh my word, Chuck, why in the world would you *do* something like that?!"

He replies, "Well, Barry had it done."

She says, "Really?!"

"Yeah!" he replies, "And different ones are doing it at school too. They do it on TV…and some singers do it too."

"Oooh", says Alice, "Well…I guess maybe I could manage to have a piece of metal ran through *my* tongue too then!"

It seems that while our knowledge rises and technology of the 21st century advances, our wisdom and morality plummets lower and lower.

Amusingly enough, do you know what slaves commonly looked like in ancient times? They were usually skinny, barely clothed and marked with tattoos and body piercings. Is that not ironic? Are not these the *same* exact things that Hollywood is constantly endorsing? Do you see what I mean then? As knowledge increases, wisdom and morality decreases. What we see in the realm of the flesh is a direct reflection of spiritual realities. And people, who are not rooted and not established in the foundation of God's word, are literally imprisoned and influenced by the "spirit" of this age.

But we, as children of God, are not called to walk according to the course and pattern of this world:

But as he which hath called you is holy, so be ye holy in all manner of conversation (I Peter 1:15).

Wherefore come out from among them, and be ye separate, saith the Lord, and touch not the unclean thing; and I will receive you. And will be a Father unto you, and ye shall be my sons and daughters, saith the Lord Almighty. Having therefore these promises, dearly beloved, let us cleanse ourselves from all filthiness of the flesh and spirit, perfecting holiness in the fear of God (II Corinthians 6:17-7:1).

What? know ye not that your body is the temple of the Holy Ghost which is in you, which ye have of God, and ye are not your own? For ye are bought with a price: therefore glorify God in your body, and in your spirit, which God's (I Corinthians 6:19-20).

Yes, there are specific things that we can do in the natural realm *here* that glorify God *there*.

Doth not even nature itself teach you, that, if a man have long hair, it is a shame unto him? But if a woman have long hair, it is a glory to her: for her hair is given her for a covering (I Corinthians 11:14-15).

In like manner also, that women adorn themselves in modest apparel, with shamefacedness and sobriety; not with broided hair, or gold, or pearls, or costly array; But (which becometh women professing godliness) with good works (I Timothy 2:9-10).

Whose adorning let it not be that outward adorning of plaiting the hair, and of wearing of gold, or of putting on of apparel; But let it be the hidden man of the heart, in that which is not corruptible, even the ornament of a meek and quiet spirit, which is in the sight of God of great price (I Peter 3:3-4).

You see, we have a higher calling than to be like everyone else. And within these passages of Scripture (listed above) are contained certain and specific things (visible signs) that identify us with God.

What separates you from the world? What active, *visible* measures are you actually taking in order to truly separate your self from everyone else? What lines are being drawn? What walls are being erected that are separating you from the rudiments of the world?

In the Old Testament there were many prophecies that were related and connected to the coming Messiah (Jesus Christ). But those that lived in the Old Testament times, even the prophets themselves, didn't fully recognize or understand them all completely. They saw them and they read them, but there were still certain things that didn't quite make perfect sense yet. For example: In Genesis 3 it was stated that a seed (a descendant) of the woman would bruise the serpent's head. What did that really mean?

In Psalm 22 David begins to graphically describe a 1st person account of a man being crucified. This was written centuries before the Romans even "invented" crucifixion.

In Isaiah 53 it describes a man being cruelly punished and beaten on behalf of the sins of nation of Israel. It didn't quite make perfect sense some 700 years before Christ.

In Zechariah 11 it talks about God naming for His price thirty pieces of silver. This was written centuries before the betrayal and crucifixion of Jesus Christ. Some people knew that these words meant something, but it was all so vague and subtle.

But when the apostles were filled with the Holy Ghost in the New Testament era, they were then supernaturally enabled to recognize, identify and connect all of these prophecies, and point out their meanings and fulfillments. But they didn't make complete sense centuries earlier. It was progressively revealed through time. Remember when Jesus was walking on the road to Emmaus with those two distraught individuals who thought that Jesus was a false hope since He was crucified and killed? The Bible says that while He walked with them, He (Jesus) opened their understanding, and beginning at Moses, He expounded unto them all the things that were written concerning Him. (See Luke 24:27.) You see, things were now, finally beginning to make sense that didn't make sense before.

Well, do you know what? There's still more information coming. The Apostle Paul said that now we see through a glass darkly. In other words, on this side of life there are still many things that we don't quite completely know or understand yet. And maybe...just maybe there's some things written that don't make complete sense right now. But someday, maybe present day obedience and faith in those things will affect eternity somehow, someway.

Paul said that the things he writes are the commandments of the Lord (see I Corinthians 14:37). Peter said that we should keep these things (his writings) *always* in remembrance (See II Peter 1:15).

So, apparently…whatever "things" we have contained and written, within our little hand-held Bibles, must be of utmost importance. So let's endeavor to visibly embrace them with all of our hearts, souls, minds…and bodies!

Chapter Eight

The Other Significance of Baptism

Often times, when we discuss the subject of baptism, we rightly do spend much time and energy conversing of the saving value of baptism. Then at other times, we may utilize much time discussing the means and the methods (by full immersion, in Jesus' name, etc.).

But I want us to consider a less-often thought about aspect of baptism. And that is the *significance* of what it actually means (or meant) when you decided to do it. What did it mean when it actually occurred? What does it mean now, today? I think that a fresh reconsidering of this *other* aspect of baptism will help play a vital role in assisting us with keeping on track with that "high call' that has been bestowed upon us.

As stated in the very first chapter of this book the nation of Israel was God's very special and chosen people. He made certain covenants with them that He didn't make with other people or nations. He gave certain promises to them than He didn't give to any other people. He even gave them certain rules, laws (commands) that they were to follow and obey that He didn't give to other nations. And it was intended by God that, through their obedience to these unique laws and commandments, the whole world would eventually become familiar with the one true God. And guess what? His plan worked! One of the main reasons that we know God or even about God is because there was (and is) a nation of Israel.

And, as mentioned earlier, we know that, even though they were God's chosen people; they did not always live in perfect submission to Him. They did not always live up to the commands and requirements of God. Remember when we discussed the vile condition that they had descended to in the Book of Isaiah 28, when it described the drunkenness of the priests? (See chapter 5 of this book if you need to refresh your memory.) Well, that scene reminds me of another passage of Scripture as well. It's found in the Book of Hosea. Notice:

Hear the word of the LORD, ye children of Israel: for the LORD hath a controversy with the inhabitants of the land, because there is no truth, nor mercy, nor knowledge of God in the land. By swearing, and lying, and killing, and stealing, and committing adultery, they break out, and blood toucheth blood... My people are destroyed for lack of knowledge: because thou hast rejected knowledge, I will also reject thee, that thou shalt be no priest to me: seeing thou hast forgotten the law of thy God, I will also forget thy children (Hosea 4:1-2, 6).

Once again we find that the nation had become so backslidden and far from God that they were about to experience His wrath. Now it's very interesting here what God says of His people here. He says that His people are "destroyed" because of their lack of knowledge (concerning Him and His Word). That's a pretty severe statement. They are *destroyed* because of their lack of knowledge.

Well, this verse reminds me of another one found in the Book of Amos. Notice this passage as well:

Behold, the days come, saith the Lord GOD, that I will send a famine in the land, not a famine of bread, nor a thirst for water, but of hearing the words of the LORD (Amos 8:11).

God warned His people here that, because of their sinfulness, a "famine" was coming. But it would not be a famine of food (bread and water), but it would be a famine of hearing (receiving) the Word of God. And naturally, of course, where there is a lack of *hearing* the Word of God then there is also going to be a lack of *blessing* as well.

Take note: We are not going to live a spiritually blessed life if we are constantly trying to dodge and evade the pervasive onslaught of truths that we will encounter when observing the Word of God. Nor will a church be blessed where the Word of God is not expounded upon or declared. Ultimately, bottom line, we either want God's ways or we don't. God has called His people (even today) to be holy, pure, undefiled, and separated from the rest of the world. Again, we have a different course to walk than everyone else does.

Now, there are many people who call themselves Christians, or children of God, who, in reality, want absolutely nothing at all to do with separation and obedience to God. They like the music of an anointed, Spirit-filled worship service. They'll gleefully dance and rejoice with everyone else in the service. They like the pastor and they like the people and the socials and the friendliness of the church. They like being prayed for when trouble comes their way. But sadly, it seems that they can't stomach truth very well. They have a hard time accepting this unavoidable fact that God has called His people, even today, to be holy.

You see, way back a long time ago in the Old Testament, in the Book of Leviticus, God said to His people, "Be ye holy, for I am Holy." (See Leviticus 11:44.) And then we find, in the New Testament, that the Apostle Peter pulled that *same* passage of Scripture (Leviticus 11:44) from the Old Testament and then he re-planted it firmly, right into the middle of New Testament Christianity. Notice:

Because it is written, Be ye holy; for I am holy (I Peter 1:16).

Even in the New Testament era, in the 21st century, we are admonished to be holy; because God is holy.

Now, I want us to notice these very important words written by the Apostle Paul:

Moreover, brethren, I would not that ye should be ignorant, how that all our fathers were under the cloud, and all passed through the sea; And were all baptized unto Moses in the cloud and in the sea (I Corinthians 10:1-2).

Remember, as discussed briefly earlier, the nation of Israel was living in bondage as slaves in the land of Egypt. But God had a plan to recue them and to *transform* them into a holy nation. The king of Egypt, however, was not so thrilled about God's plan. He resisted God and the man of God (Moses). And so God began to send several awful plagues upon the land of Egypt. And every time that the king would refuse to let God's people go, the Lord would send another plague. He sent locusts, He sent flies, and He sent frogs and darkness. The waters even turned to blood. And finally, the last plague came: Death on the first-born of every man and beast in the entire nation.

Well, finally the king conceded, and he said, in essence, "Get out of here!" And all looked well for the nation of Israel…until a few days later. They were now camped at the shores of the Red Sea. And the Egyptian army was quickly closing in and approaching from behind. The king had changed his mind. And with no where to turn, God instructed Moses to extend his staff over the sea. And when he obeyed, the sea miraculously parted and Israel went safely through the divided waters. But when the Egyptians followed, the waters collapsed and they were drowned.

So here were God's people, safely rejoicing on the other side of the sea. They were free! Egypt was buried under the sea and was no longer a threat! Now, notice again:

Moreover, brethren, I would not that ye should be ignorant, how that all our fathers were under the cloud, and all passed through the sea; And were all baptized unto Moses in the cloud and in the sea (I Corinthians 10:1-2).

You see, when the nation of Israel marched through that divided sea it was good bye to slavery! Goodbye bondage! Goodbye oppression! And, according to the Apostle Paul, this crossing of the Red Sea was a "type" of water baptism today. It was a point (moment) of separation and cleansing. Now notice these words also:

Know ye not, that so many of us as were baptized into Jesus Christ were baptized into his death? Therefore we are buried with him by baptism into death: that like as Christ was raised

up from the dead by the glory of the Father, even so we also should walk in newness of life. For if we have been planted together in the likeness of his death, we shall be also in the likeness of his resurrection: Knowing this, that our old man is crucified with him, that the body of sin might be destroyed, that henceforth we should not serve sin (Romans 6:3-6).

Let me put this very plainly: When you are baptized, and you go down, into (under) the water, it's goodbye to the old life! It's goodbye to the ungodly habits. It's goodbye to self-will. It's goodbye to ungodliness. Can I get plain? It's goodbye to the alcohol (booze). Notice these warnings of Solomon:

Wine is a mocker, strong drink is raging: and whosoever is deceived thereby is not wise (Proverbs 20:1).

Who hath woe? who hath sorrow? who hath contentions? who hath babbling? who hath wounds without cause? who hath redness of eyes? They that tarry long at the wine; they that go to seek mixed wine. Look not thou upon the wine when it is red, when it giveth his colour in the cup, when it moveth itself aright. At the last it biteth

like a serpent, and stingeth like an adder. Thine eyes shall behold strange women, and thine heart shall utter perverse things. Yea, thou shalt be as he that lieth down in the midst of the sea, or as he that lieth upon the top of a mast. They have stricken me, shalt thou say, and I was not sick; they have beaten me, and I felt it not: when shall I awake? I will seek it yet again (Proverbs 20:1).

Notice what Paul said of this as well:

Know ye not that the unrighteous shall not inherit the kingdom of God? Be not deceived: neither fornicators, nor idolaters, nor adulterers, nor effeminate, nor abusers of themselves with mankind, Nor thieves, nor covetous, nor drunkards, nor revilers, nor extortioners, shall inherit the kingdom of God. And such were some of you: but ye are washed, but ye are sanctified, but ye are justified in the name of the Lord Jesus, and by the Spirit of our God (I Corinthians 6:9-11).

"And be not drunk with wine, wherein is excess..." (Ephesians 5:18).

You see, when you go down into (under) the water, it's goodbye to the tobacco! And goodbye to the drugs! It's goodbye to the sexual promiscuity, etc. No, we (baptized children of God) don't live with our boyfriends or our girlfriends, etc. We don't continue on in sexual immorality (fornication or adultery). No, these things are gone.

However, when you come up, *out* of the water, it's hello to salvation! It's hello to hope! It's hello to living right! It's hello to spiritual freedom!

Basically, when you get baptized, it's good bye to the old life, and it's hello to the new life! This needs to be our attitude *before* we're baptized and it needs to *stay* our attitude long *after* we're baptized.

Notice these words in the Book of Ephesians:

This I say therefore, and testify in the Lord, that ye henceforth walk not as other Gentiles walk, in the vanity of their mind, Having the understanding darkened, being alienated from the life of God through the ignorance that is in them, because of the blindness of their heart: Who being past feeling have given themselves over unto lasciviousness, to work all uncleanness with greediness. But ye have not so learned Christ; If so be that ye have heard him, and have been taught by him, as the truth is in Jesus: That ye put off

concerning the former conversation the old man, which is corrupt according to the deceitful lusts; And be renewed in the spirit of your mind; And that ye put on the new man, which after God is created in righteousness and true holiness (Ephesians 4:17-24).

Let me say this, when you repent of your sins and you are baptized in Jesus' name, it doesn't mean that you have now become perfect. We will still fight, we will make mistakes, we will fall, and we will fail at times. But when we do, I believe that it's good and beneficial for us to look back at the significance of our baptism; that landmark in time. And it's good to remember again that "dying" moment and that undying dedication and to reactivate its meaning again.

It was at that point in time that you publicly, visibly professed and claimed your acceptance of God and His will in your life. It was more than a mere ritual or routine. It was a departing from Egypt, so to speak. It was a departure from worldliness and worldly behavior, and worldly thinking. It was a spiritual renewal commencing a life of holiness and righteousness.

The like figure whereunto even baptism doth also now save us (not the putting away of the filth of the flesh, but the answer of a good conscience toward God,) by the resurrection of Jesus Christ (I Peter 3:21).

Your baptism was your answer (response) to a call from God to forsake all else and to attach yourself entirely (body and soul) to His will and His Word. May you remain ever faithful to that call all the days of your life. May you ever be a "beauty" in the eyes of *your* Beholder. Amen.

Endnotes

Chapter One
1. This was shared in a sermon delivered by Rev. B.J. Wilmoth in Sacramento, CA.
2. http://www.christadelphiansisters.org/modesty.htm (By Loanne Clements).
3. *More Hot Illustrations for Youth Talks*, Wayne Rice (Zondervan Publishing House, Grand Rapids, Michigan) page 58. (As retold in *The Prudence Awakening* by Darin Bowler page 18).

Chapter Two
1. http://www.reflectingalife.com/2012/04/12/45
2. *The New Analytical Greek Lexicon*, Wesley J. Perschbacher (Hendrickson Publishers, Peabody, Massachusetts).
3. *Power Before the Throne*, Ruth Rieder (Morris Publishing, Kearney Nebraska).

Chapter Three
1. *Handbook of Today's Religions*, Josh McDowell and Don Stewart, (Thomas Nelson Publishers, Nashville, Tennessee) Page 237-238.

2. *Webster's New World Dictionary*, (The World Publishing Company, Cleveland and New York).

3. *Reflecting the Glory*, Ruth Rieder (Morris Publishing, Kearney Nebraska) Page 78.

4. *The New Analytical Greek Lexicon*, Wesley J. Perschbacher (Hendrickson Publishers, Peabody, Massachusetts).

Chapter five

1. http://www.sarathi.org/WrittenStories/telegraphOperator.htm

2. *The New Analytical Greek Lexicon*, Wesley J. Perschbacher (Hendrickson Publishers, Peabody, Massachusetts).

3. *The Expanded Vine's Expository Dictionary of New Testament Words*, W.E. Vine (Bethany House Publishers, Minneapolis, Minnesota).

4. This was shared in a lesson taught by Rev. Delton Fair in Lodi, CA.

5. *In Bonds of Love*, Nathaniel J. Wilson (Reach Worldwide Inc., Sacramento, California) Page 144.

Chapter Six

1. *What a Difference a Line Can Make*, Larry L. Booker (Lighthouse Publications, Rialto, California) Page 138-140.

Notes

Notes

Notes

Notes

CPSIA information can be obtained
at www.ICGtesting.com
Printed in the USA
BVHW061429221219
567503BV00009B/839/P